UNVEILING TAROT

78 catalysts for personal awakening

LAURA SHAW

PEAK LIFE PRESS

ALSO BY LAURA SHAW

Unveiling Tarot Journal

ISBN 979-8-9862639-1-5 Paperback

ISBN 979-8-9862639-0-8 Ebook

peaklifepress.com

For Audrey and Aria

CONTENTS

PART ONE
AWAKENING THROUGH TAROT

WORKING WITH THE CARDS	5
The Archetypal Tarot Journey	6
HOW THIS BOOK WORKS	9
DEVELOPING A RELATIONSHIP WITH YOUR CARDS	11
Choosing A Deck	12
READING FOR SELF AND OTHERS	13

PART TWO
HOW TO STUDY TAROT FOR AWAKENING

STORING & HANDLING YOUR DECK	19
THE THREE-CARD DAILY DRAW	23
FREE WILL TAROT	25
ELEMENTS & SUITS	27
Pentacles & Earth	27
Swords & Air	27
Cups & Water	28
Wands & Fire	28
NUMBERS & TAROT	29
UPRIGHT & REVERSED CARDS	33

PART THREE
THE MAJOR ARCANA

0. THE FOOL	37
Reversed Fool	38
Activating the Fool	39
1-7 FOUNDATIONAL LESSONS	41
1. MAGICIAN	43
Reversed Magician	44
Activating the Magician	45
2. HIGH PRIESTESS	47
Reversed High Priestess	49
Activating the High Priestess	50
3. EMPRESS	51
Reversed Empress	53
Activating the Empress	54
4. EMPEROR	55
Reversed Emperor	57
Activating the Emperor	58
5. HIEROPHANT	59
Reversed Hierophant	61
Activating the Hierophant	62
6. LOVERS	63
Reversed Lovers	65
Activating the Lovers	66
7. CHARIOT	67
Reversed Chariot	68
Activating the Chariot	69
8-14 TRANSFORMATION & EVOLUTION	71
8. STRENGTH	73
Reversed Strength	74
Activating Strength	77

9. THE HERMIT   79
Reversed Hermit   81
Activating the Hermit   81

10. WHEEL OF FORTUNE   83
Reversed Wheel of Fortune   84
Activating Wheel of Fortune   85

11. JUSTICE   87
Reversed Justice   89
Activating Justice   89

12. HANGED MAN   91
Reversed Hanged Man   92
Activating Hanged Man   94

13. DEATH   95
Reversed Death   96
Activating Death   98

14. TEMPERANCE   99
Reversed Temperance   100
Activating Temperance   101

15-21 EXISTENTIAL LESSONS   103

15. DEVIL   105
Reversed Devil   107
Activating the Devil   108

16. TOWER   109
Reversed Tower   110
Activating the Tower   111

17. STAR   113
Reversed Star   114
Activating the Star   115

18. MOON   117
Reversed Moon   118
Activating the Moon   120

19. SUN   121
Reversed Sun   122
Activating the Sun   123

20. JUDGMENT   125
Reversed Judgment   126
Activating Judgment   127

21. THE WORLD   129
Reversed World   130
Activating the World   131

PART FOUR
THE MINOR ARCANA

ACE   135
Ace of Pentacles   135
Ace of Swords   137
Ace of Cups   139
Ace of Wands   141

TWO   143
Two of Pentacles   143
Two of Swords   145
Two of Cups   147
Two of Wands   149

THREE   153
Three of Pentacles   153
Three of Swords   155
Three of Cups   157
Three of Wands   159

FOUR   163
Four of Pentacles   163
Four of Swords   166
Four of Cups   168
Four of Wands   170

FIVE 173
Five of Pentacles 173
Five of Swords 175
Five of Cups 178
Five of Wands 179

SIX 183
Six of Pentacles 183
Six of Swords 185
Six of Cups 187
Six of Wands 189

SEVEN 191
Seven of Pentacles 191
Seven of Swords 193
Seven of Cups 195
Seven of Wands 197

EIGHT 201
Eight of Pentacles 201
Eight of Swords 203
Eight of Cups 206
Eight of Wands 208

NINE 211
Nine of Pentacles 211
Nine of Swords 214
Nine of Cups 216
Nine of Wands 218

TEN 221
Ten of Pentacles 221
Ten of Swords 223
Ten of Cups 225
Ten of Wands 227

COURT CARDS 231
Pages 232
Knights 242
Queens 251
Kings 259

CONCLUSION   271

Card Spreads   273
Acknowledgments   281
About the Author   283

PART ONE

AWAKENING THROUGH TAROT

How can flat rectangles of paper with simple pictures on them help you see your life in more dimensions?

When I began studying tarot, my life went from flat to multidimensional. From black and white to vivid technicolor.

Time became bendable, reality became fluid, and ice cream never tasted so good.

Somehow, these rectangles of paper woke me up to something that was always there, but I'd forgotten.

This can happen for you too.

Unveiling Tarot isn't like other tarot books where you look up the meaning of cards and memorize them. In this book, the cards become a customized catalyst for your awakening.

If you approach tarot in the manner described in this book, you'll experience the meaning of the cards personally, and the cards will deeply inform your life.

Exploring the cards sequentially and organically allows your life to automatically teach you about each card. It's uncanny, but also thrilling, to see how invoking the cards can transform your life with no more effort than intention and willingness.

You may heal an intimate relationship when you contemplate the Lovers card. Or you may have a power struggle at work with your narcissistic boss as you engage with the Emperor card. One student became pregnant when she studied the High Priestess and the Empress cards.

Meaningful tarot reading goes beyond rote memorization. It requires practice and a personal relationship with each card.

The way most of us were expected to learn in school only engages us mentally. This approach to tarot is focused on integrated learning. I'm inviting you to pay close attention to your life, your patterns, the moment, your body, and your feelings. Approaching tarot this way allows you to be touched and transformed by your relationship with the cards. It's not something you can control, but something you participate with. When you develop your relationship with the cards in this personal, experiential way, the wisdom you gain will be strong and transformative.

Deep transformation takes time to integrate, so be patient with your process. Much of your awakening will be done while you sleep. Over time, all the little bits will add up. And don't worry if you fall off your practice for a time. When you return, you'll likely realize you were busy living your tarot lesson.

MY AWAKENING THROUGH TAROT

After reading the little pamphlet that came with my first deck of tarot cards until it fell apart, I finally found Marlene Delott, who became my tarot teacher and spiritual mother. This was before the internet, so finding a teacher was its own kind of pilgrimage.

I first studied in a small class with other students of varying degrees of familiarity with tarot and the occult, as it was called back in the 80s. I approached tarot with the same tools that made me academically successful, but it didn't work.

Well, it worked a little. I understood the religious, psychological and numerological symbolism, but only on a mental level. The knowledge of the archetypes wasn't integrated in my life or in my body.

One woman in class knew how to read a crystal ball. Another was a nationally sought-after astrologer. Out of my depth and overwhelmed, I desperately wanted to access tarot's secret language too.

Then one day I was jogging, and a man walked by with two giant Poodles on leashes. The Poodle on his left was white, and the Poodle on his right was black. I laughed as I recognized the Chariot card. For a moment, something opened inside me to let the light crack through. And then it shut.

Later that week, I met my friend for lunch. She was seven months pregnant and wearing a red maternity business suit with big gold buttons. While she ate chocolate cream pie for dessert, she raised her fork and I saw the Empress. That time I felt the hair on the back of my neck stand up.

After those two incidents, I entered a phase of quickening, with flutters of awareness and transformation involving more real life tarot. It was as if the coding of the universe became visible and then melted. I finally had some clues about how to get beyond my limited approach to experiencing life.

A lot of other less fun things accompanied this awakening. A painful and dramatic breakup, a crash of my car, sickness, moving, financial struggle and other Tower and Death card themes as I detoxed my limited beliefs and integrated my new awareness.

Eventually I found my way, but I wish I'd had someone to simplify the material and make it applicable to daily life. I wish I'd had a safe container as I woke up.

My hope in writing this book is to offer you a safe container for your unique process of awakening through tarot.

I don't believe it's possible to teach you tarot. The premise of this approach is to have a direct experience of the cards for yourself on your personal path of awakening. I invite you to look at the cards in a spirit of discovery, to understand how they directly relate to what is happening in your life.

With this approach, your knowledge of tarot will be rooted in your real life, in real time, and tarot will organically unveil itself to you and transform your life.

PREPARING TO AWAKEN

As you awaken on this spiritual plane, your body also awakens. It's common to experience physical symptoms as your body detoxes and clears out memories, old patterns, and limiting beliefs at a cellular level. Most people need to sleep more, often with potent dreams.

It's not unusual for relationships to become healthier or fall off if they no longer serve you. Your work may change as you gain more clarity about who you are.

As you awaken with tarot, you may become more aware of subtle energies, and your innate psychic abilities will strengthen as a natural byproduct of your growth and newfound knowledge.

Another welcome effect of studying tarot is that the world becomes more beautiful. You may belly laugh more and hear music in new ways. As your heart awakens, you naturally develop more tolerance and compassion for others.

Some days, awakening is fun and empowering. Other days, it can be intense and challenging. You may have to cry on and off for three months, or you may feel you're losing it as belief systems are dismantled and your perception of reality shifts.

Breathing and body-centered practices such as yoga or walking can help you integrate. Or simply bringing awareness to your body can help, such as feeling your feet.

When it gets hard, try to remember that you are integrating a higher threshold of awareness and surrender to the process. Ultimately, awakening is the work that matters most.

Working with the Cards

TAROT OFFERS a safe and gentle tool for personal growth and self-discovery. The tarot cards function like a mirror to know yourself more completely, especially the shadowy parts that prefer to operate behind the scenes.

Bringing awareness to these unseen aspects allows you to connect and integrate all aspects of yourself and to transcend your limitations.

Diving into the cards can help you see the archetypal and universal forces you are reckoning with. In this way, tarot can offer some comfort in your suffering, not from an ability to predict or control an outcome, but from having compassion for your human experience.

The potent combination of intention, willingness, plus the archetypal images on tarot cards can bypass your ego's defenses and cut straight through to the blueprint of who you are and why you're here.

Once your ego has stepped aside, you are at the ground zero of existence. Your old stories and false beliefs fall off, and you automatically live your life with more synchronicity, ease, and joy.

THE ARCHETYPAL TAROT JOURNEY

The Fool represents the "player" of the game of tarot. The game is the Fool's journey. Of the 22 major arcana (secrets or mysteries) cards, the Fool represents both the beginning and the end, hence the Fool card is numbered "0".

The remaining 21 major arcana cards can be divided into three groups of seven cards, with each group reflecting the three main stages of human development: Socialization, Morality, and Existence.

———

SOCIALIZATION: MAGICIAN TO THE CHARIOT

The first stage of the Fool's journey is the socialization stage. This stage is about growing up, being socialized and getting out into the world.

MORALITY: STRENGTH TO TEMPERANCE

The second developmental phase is about morality and recognizing how your actions influence others. This is where you're changing your stories and belief systems.

EXISTENCE: DEVIL TO THE WORLD

The third stage of the major arcana is existential. It involves living a life aligned with universal truth.

———

Life isn't a perfectly sequential experience, and the cards don't show up in your daily draws this way either. However, I still recommend studying the cards in order, beginning with the Fool, because it provides a clearer understanding of how the major arcana cards represent the full spectrum of human experience.

Each of the minor arcana suits tell a story, beginning with the Ace and culminating with the Ten. If you are brand new to tarot, it is important to begin by looking at the cards in their original sequence to familiarize yourself with the arc of experience the cards illustrate.

How this Book Works

1. First, read the description of each card starting with the Fool and ending with King of Wands. This sequence reflects a developmental journey as the cards build on each other.
2. At the end of each card's description, there is an Activating section, with an invitation to integrate the lesson of the card.
3. The questions can be used both as journal prompts to go deeper and as affirmations to activate the card's energy in your life.
4. For maximum benefit, I recommend developing a relationship with the cards based on your impressions and connecting them with what you experience in your life first before researching outside interpretations.
5. Start with the Three-Card Daily Draw and give yourself at least nine months to a year of regular practice.
6. Try to hold off on reading for others until you have your own sense of the cards, at least a few lunar cycles. This is because when you are just starting, it's hard to hold your center and access your knowing in the presence of another. The need to perform or the other person's needs can block your inner voice.

THE GOAL of this style of tarot study is awakening, not to become a better reader for others. Many people study tarot with no intention of ever reading for others. If you would like to read for others, or already read for others, becoming a better tarot reader will automatically happen.

Developing a Relationship
with Your Cards

YOU CAN EXPERIENCE your cards by simply gazing at the cards with curiosity, noticing, for example, that there is snow on the Hermit card. Or, observing that the Sun card gives a sense of warmth and exudes happiness.

Or maybe you'll wonder what's up with the floating cup on the Four of Cups card and wonder why isn't that person taking the cup that is being offered?

You can engage in a conversation with the card itself, particularly if it is dogging you, or represents an issue with which you're struggling. You can ask the card questions, such as...

- What are you about?
- How can I learn from you?
- What are you trying to show me?

When you meet each card like you would a new friend without conditions or preconceived notions, you'll develop a deep understanding of the cards that is uniquely yours and you'll never have to look up what a card means because you'll automatically know.

CHOOSING A DECK

Here's how to choose a deck to work with on your tarot journey:

- The standard teaching deck is the Rider-Waite-Smith. This deck will work best with the approach in this book.
- This deck was co-created by academic and mystic, A.E. Waite and illustrated by Pamela Coleman Smith. Both were members of the Hermetic Order of the Golden Dawn, a secret society dedicated to the study of metaphysics and the occult.
- Originally published in 1909 by the Rider Company, the Rider-Waite-Smith deck isn't inclusive, but forms the foundation for most other decks.
- The tarot community is actively evolving to become more diverse and equitable. There are now hundreds of inclusive decks to choose from.
- The author consciously chose gender inclusivity in this book. Figures in the original deck are male/female, but this book validates that human experience transcends those limited binaries.
- If you're not comfortable with the Rider-Waite-Smith deck, then choose one that speaks to you aesthetically, intuitively, and energetically.
- For the purposes of this book, it's best if the deck you use follows the pattern of 22 major arcana.
- It doesn't matter if the names of the major arcana cards don't match because the numbers and universal development cycle will correlate.

Reading for Self and Others

THE GOAL for this approach to tarot is to gain insight. If you have a troubling situation in your life, you can use tarot to understand how you may be contributing to your own suffering and what you can learn from the situation. It can also validate what's working well and help you identify your strengths and best opportunities.

One key to getting the most out of tarot reading is understanding how to phrase your questions. Most people seek tarot readings because they want answers, but if you ask a poorly worded question, the answer you receive will likely be confusing.

In a tarot reading, the most effective questions are open-ended and incorporate words such as Why, How, and What if? Close-ended, specific outcome, or yes/no questions such as, "Will I be a rockstar?" are limiting. You can miss the complexity of the answer, plus it can be unethical and violate free will by tipping into prediction.

For example, instead of asking about a prognosis of a sick family member, you can look at your relationship with the sick family member and see what major life lessons and themes you both are dealing with. Or ask how to best support them during this trying time.

Instead of trying to answer loaded and limited questions such as, 'Should I quit my job?' ask for the name of the company and the job title and then focus on that while shuffling and drawing the cards. In this way, when you lay out the cards, you can see the full picture and life lessons surrounding their current job situation.

Maybe there are sabotaging or limiting behaviors, or maybe they've manifested their same family dynamics in the workplace. Sometimes, quitting the job won't help because it will be the same story in the next place.

When there is a question about another person, such as a romantic interest, friend or family member, I'll ask for the person's name and birthdate, if known, and then have the person for whom I'm reading focus on that person while they shuffle and draw cards.

The cards will then provide a snapshot of the dynamic with that person. For example, maybe you have a major crush on someone. Instead of trying to answer whether they are your soulmate, you can simply think about the person and then draw cards. Many times it's been a wake up call when the crushing client doesn't even register in the cards.

When looking at your dynamics with other people, you can gain an understanding of what is motivating them, where they are coming from, and what life lessons they are working on. If you're struggling in an intimate partnership, for example, and you look at your partner and see how they felt smothered and responsible for their mother and as a result has unresolved anger toward women, then you can better understand how that dynamic could play into your relationship.

The cards will show the dynamics at play with any situation. In this way, you can see patterns and make genuine change.

If there is a question about starting a business, then focus on the business idea or name and then draw cards. If there is a potential business partner involved, look at the relationship dynamic with that person by focusing on the potential business partner and then drawing cards.

In my early days, I moonlighted as a tarot reader at parties. One hostess hired me for the same Halloween party for three consecutive years. At one of these parties, a middle-aged, nicely dressed man consulted with me.

He sat down stiffly and tested me with a poker face. Although an adversarial stance isn't the most productive use of a tarot consultation, everyone needs to do what they need to do in order to feel comfortable and this guy needed some proof I was legit.

I drew a few cards and the Knight of Pentacles came up reversed. "It looks like you're considering an investment and it doesn't look good. You'll likely lose money." To be clear, the Knight of Pentacles doesn't always represent money, but I could tell from his presence and his attitude he probably wasn't thinking about pilates or planting an organic vegetable garden, plus he had the Fool card reversed and the King of Cups card reversed.

"This guy is somehow involved" and I held up the King of Cups card reversed while I described the type of person he represented.

Once I passed his test, he asked me directly about the business venture he was considering. Since he was thinking about going into a partnership, we looked at the partner and how it would be to work together. It didn't look good.

There was a Seven of Swords meaning there was something fishy and his potential business partner came up again as the King of Cups reversed, with the Devil upright and the Seven of Cups reversed. It looked like potential addiction issues and empty promises. Besides the Fool reversed, the key card that drove the nail into the coffin for this guy's business hopes was the Knight of Pentacles reversed.

I never directly advised him about the business, because I'm not qualified. I only described what I saw in the cards, which was an amplification and affirmation of what he already knew on some level. He remained poker-faced throughout the reading, thanked me perfunctorily, then left.

Parties are a great way to become a strong tarot reader. You get exposed to many people in a short time and you have to connect and communicate something meaningful in five to ten minutes.

When reading tarot at parties, you realize quickly you can't care about anyone's response or opinion of you. Often, you can be spot on with your reading, but the person isn't ready to hear it and instead kills the messenger by making the tarot reader wrong.

It's happened more than once where the miffed partygoer shares the "totally ridiculous" reading with their friends at the party, only to have their friends affirm they see the same thing, often privately thanking me for calling out a major issue in this person's life.

The next year, they invited me to read tarot at the annual party and the same guy showed up, much more open this time. He handed me $20 and said, "Do you remember last year when I was going to start a business?" I remembered. "Well, you saved me $200,000. You were absolutely right about that guy!"

At the end of the book, there are explanations of basic spreads that can be used when reading for others.

PART TWO

HOW TO STUDY TAROT
FOR AWAKENING

Storing & Handling Your Deck

It's best to not let anyone else touch your deck at first. The reason for this is that you want to have only your energy on your deck while you're developing a relationship with your cards. I recommend waiting at least one moon cycle, ideally three.

There are many opinions about the "right" way to store and to use your cards. I've found that the key is to be respectful, like you would with any other item of value. Many people have a specially designated area, like a special drawer, shelf or box where they keep their deck.

I recommend wrapping your cards in a silk scarf, or using a silk-lined bag to help contain the energy. Silk has a natural energetic matrix that protects the energy of the cards. If you're vegan, a natural fiber such as cotton or bamboo is a good choice. You can sleep with your deck under your pillow for extra subconscious activation.

Sometimes your tarot deck may need to be "cleared" or "cleansed" of energetic debris. I'll often clear my deck when I'm doing back-to-back readings at a party where many people are touching the cards.

I can tell when I need to clear a deck when certain cards get "hot", meaning that they are repeatedly drawn despite thorough shuffling. The "hot" cards will espouse the zeitgeist of the party, but the repetition creates a magnetism that pulls people to draw them, and then the reading isn't as accurate.

When this occurs, I'll switch out decks, giving the other deck time to rest and reset. I may also spray cleansing mist (about 35 drops of sage, rosemary or cedar essential oil in a spray bottle with water and a little alcohol as a preservative) to further clear the energy. Sometimes I'll simply knock with my knuckles on the deck three times, blow on the deck, or place a quartz crystal on top of the deck to help the deck clear and reboot.

Now and then, I put the cards in their original order. This is like coming home for the cards and allows them to deeply reset.

You can also charge or infuse them by intentionally leaving them in a powerful environment. A fun way to do this is by giving them a moon bath. You leave the cards face up near a window where moonlight enters to energetically "soak" in the moon's energy. Use a new moon for charging and a full moon for cleansing.

In the summer, I'll leave my cards outside in the sunlight or moonlight for a bit, but not overnight. They're paper after all and can be damaged by moisture.

Particularly powerful times to charge your cards are during the summer and winter solstices or the spring and fall equinoxes.

These recommendations, however, are optional and unnecessary. It is possible to block authentic experience if you put too much ritualization into the process. True presence in your body and in the moment will allow you to tap into your ultimate wisdom.

There is no right or wrong way to shuffle. If traditional shuffling doesn't work for you, the cards can be fanned out faced down, Vegas style, with cards chosen from the array.

It's helpful to have a consistent way of cutting and shuffling because it puts you in the mindset of reading, like priming a pump. However, there is also an argument to be made for randomness because it can be more in-the-moment. You'll find whatever way is right for you. The cards only care if you care.

This is how I have been shuffling and cutting for 30 years:

1. Ensure that the deck is fully shuffled. There are 78 cards, so this could take seven or eight shuffles minimum.
2. If reading for someone else, establish before you turn over the cards if the cards will face you or if they will face the person for whom you're reading.
3. Using the left hand, cut the deck twice, forming three piles.
4. Pick up the piles of cards using the right hand, starting from the farthest right pile of cards and stacking it on top of the next two piles so that the first cut ends up on top of the deck.
5. Cut one more time using the left hand and stacking with your right hand.
6. Use your right hand to lay out the cards.

In esoteric traditions, the left side is associated with the occult. The right hand is the dominant hand for the majority and it's thought the use of the right hand may limit non-linear experience. The left side is correlated with the right hemisphere of the brain which is the creative and artistic side.

If you're not accustomed to using your left hand, you will need to pay more attention while cutting the deck, which strengthens the reading. If you're left-handed, follow the same process.

Since cards have different meanings when they are upright or reversed, you'll want to turn each of the cards over consistently. I turn mine over from the side so they remain facing the same way they were in the deck.

I prefer to read with the cards facing the person for whom I'm reading because the images communicate directly to their subconscious, but reading upside down can be hard at first.

There are no mistakes with tarot. When a card flies out of the deck while you're shuffling, or falls on the floor while you're laying them out, pay attention to what the card is trying to show you. However, if a whole chunk of the deck falls on the floor because they are awkward to shuffle, don't worry about it.

THE THREE-CARD DAILY DRAW

ONE OF THE best ways to learn is to draw three cards every day and notice what you notice. The most ideal times are early in the morning, before you begin your day, or late at night, before bed. At these times, the ego is less engaged and there is greater access to the subconscious.

However, doing it at any time is better than not doing it at all.

Jotting down the date and the cards you drew is enough, but adding any observations or notations about what is going on in your life in a dedicated tarot journal is the most optimal approach.

Over time and with consistent practice, you'll notice patterns and will make connections with events and experiences in your life.

Shuffle and cut the cards in whatever way feels right for you.

Lay out three cards in the following order:

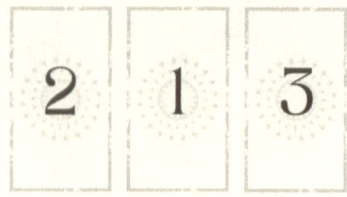

1. card in the center = present
2. card to the left = recent past
3. card to the right = near future

A. Jot down which cards you drew in your tarot notebook.

B. Note if the cards are upside down or right side up. If you get any Kings, Queens, Knights, or Pages, try to guess who in your life they may represent.

C. Note any impressions that you receive from the cards and also anything interesting going on in your life.

D. Notice if any cards fall or 'jump' out of the deck, or repeatedly show up in your daily draw. These have significance.

E. Try not to research what the cards mean until you've formed your own impressions.

Free Will Tarot

For many people, tarot reading is thought of as fortune-telling, where predictions of the future are made. In these cases, the underlying motivation for a personal study of tarot is a desire to know and thus control the future.

Prediction is disempowering, distracting, and can be dangerous. I've seen it go wrong, and it isn't worth it. Predictions, good or bad, can echo in your mind and block your authentic experience. The truth is, we have free will and choice.

When you read for others, they will often ask you to predict for them. Don't do it. The moment you predict for someone else, you've made yourself their source.

You are not in charge of anyone else's life, and it can put both of you in a confusing position and damage the relationship. This is an important boundary to maintain.

When you find yourself accurately "seeing the future", it is because you can see deeply embedded patterns and life lessons being played out. Helping yourself or the person for whom you're reading to understand and, where possible, change unhelpful patterns is the point of tarot.

The cards reflect the mindset at the moment they were drawn. Once awareness is brought to an issue during a reading, the person's mindset can change, resulting in a different outcome.

Many times, a problematic situation will be transformed after a reading. This is when tarot is awesome. No more action needed. Awareness is the ultimate cure.

Elements & Suits

THE EASIEST WAY TO increase your understanding of tarot is to memorize the four elements that correlate with the four suits. The elements of earth, air, water and fire correspond with the suits of pentacles, swords, cups and wands. Bearing these correspondences in mind when interpreting the card will instantly increase your reading by 50%. Listed below are some of the topics that apply to the element.

PENTACLES & EARTH

Physicality, body, finance, fertility, growth, stuck, health, foundation, land, real estate, work, grounded, nutrition, sleeping, exercise, self-care, business, security

SWORDS & AIR

Thoughts, judgements, decisions, knowledge, mental health, stress, anguish, worry, wisdom, intelligence, discernment, the psychological state, stress, communication

CUPS & WATER

Relationships, passion, emotions, flowing, overflowing, flooding, circulation, frozen, addiction, manipulation, delusion, creativity, cleansing, depression, avoidance of emotion

WANDS & FIRE

Inspiration, stress, success, anger, sexual energy, ideas, realization, struggle, fighting, creativity, will, business, innovation, invention, motivation

Numbers & Tarot

EXCEPT FOR THE COURT CARDS, each card has a number. Numbers have great significance in tarot and are the foundation of the mystical study of Numerology.

Numerology is based on the teachings of Pythagoras (c. 570–495 BCE), a mathematician and philosopher in Ancient Greece who believed that numbers could unlock the secrets of the universe.

Each of the numbers has its own symbolism, meaning, and personality. The specific vibration of each number influences our lives in different ways.

A dive into Numerology can be informative and complement the study of tarot. Mary Greer's, *Tarot for Yourself* is an excellent resource if you'd like to learn more about the correlation of numbers with tarot. A quick search on the internet can tell you your Life Path number and your Personal Year number.

Knowing that you're in a 9 personal year, for example, will provide a context for the loss and letting go of what you are likely experiencing as you complete the 9-year cycle.

Besides the list below, each of the 9 numbers is described in the introduction to minor arcana. The numerological significance will be helpful to keep in mind when interpreting cards.

It's also helpful to note any preponderance of numbers in readings. If there are multiple aces (number 1) and the Magician card (which is number 1 in the major arcana), for example, then it would signify new beginnings in multiple areas of your life.

1 - A beginning, pioneer, seeds, fresh start, breaking new ground, new frontiers, the self, the ego

2 - Relationship, choices, balance, cooperation, intimacy, harmony, partnerships, duality, attraction, conflict

3 - Communication, curiosity, creativity, communication, growth, fertility, celebration, connection, teaching, expression

4 - Stability, organization, security, structure, container, pragmatism, concrete, building, power, status

5 - Instability, conflict, fighting, loss, freedom, variety, curiosity, chaos, travel, change, new experiences

6 - Community, relationships, social responsibility, caring for others, family, nostalgia, home, social recognition of success

7 - Introspection, soul-searching, perseverance, patience, truth seeking, magic, luck, strategy, analysis, wisdom, challenge, victory

8 - Harvesting the fruits of success, strength, achievement, culmination, business, executive, leader, mastery, authority

9 - Completion, outcome, endings, loss, letting go, humanitarian, big picture, reflection, wisdom, satisfaction, fulfillment, relief

10 - (1 + 0 = 1) the completion of a cycle and a new beginning. Rebirth, renewal, excess and extremes, ultimate culmination but also containing the seeds of the next cycle.

Upright & Reversed Cards

Reversed cards add a layer of complexity to tarot that can feel overwhelming when you're first learning. Reversals are not essential to this specific method of engaging with tarot. The reader is welcome to skip the reversals entirely and read the upright only.

Each card represents an entire spectrum of ways in which a person can come into or go out of balance. The cards have different meanings when reversed, but will carry the same essential category of lesson whether upright or reversed.

It's helpful to think of a reversed card as having either the opposite meaning of the upright version, or else an intensified meaning of the upright version.

For example, the Two of Swords upright can mean needing to exercise choice, but when it is reversed, it can mean that a decision was made. Or, in its reversed and intensified version, it can mean active avoidance of making a decision or that the decision was taken out of your hands. In which case, you become the passive recipient of the change you sought to evade.

If the reversals feel too complicated, just focus on the upright interpretations. You can always review and add in the reversals later.

PART THREE

THE MAJOR ARCANA

The major arcana represent universal life lessons. The Fool begins and ends the journey through the 21 major arcana.

Each of the major arcana cards builds upon the card before it and charts the development of human consciousness, beginning with the awakening of power in the Magician card, to the hard-won wisdom in the Hermit card. Then plummeting through the destruction of limiting belief systems in the Tower card, and finally to the fully realized consciousness of the World card.

I was at a Renaissance festival where a tarot reader removed the minor arcana from her deck and used only the major arcana cards to read for people. This was a smart approach, especially in a festival setting where she had to cut quickly to the root issues in order to supply a meaningful reading.

When major arcana cards show up, they trump all the other cards, because they show the major life lessons being processed. I recommend studying and paying the most attention to the major arcana cards. They will always show the driving forces to which the minor arcana are responding.

0. The Fool

Element: Air

New beginning, opportunity, possibility, potential, optimism

If tarot were a board game, the Fool would represent the player. In tarot, the Fool is considered the beginning and also the end of the major arcana which is why it is numbered "0."

On the card, a youthful figure is setting off into the world to seek fame and fortune. The Fool carries a small sack and is standing on the edge of a precipice, gazing up.

Idealism is depicted, but there is also ignorance and the arrogance of youth as the figure is heedless of the dangers lurking just one small step in the wrong direction.

The Fool card is hopeful with a bright yellow background. They hold a white flower, symbolizing hope, idealism and purity of intent. The sun shines brightly and a white dog nips at their heels.

The white dog symbolizes undeveloped animal instinct and trying to keep this idealistic character grounded. There is an immense mountain in the background, symbolic of the Fool's possibility and ambition.

Maybe you're starting a new job or want to launch a new business venture. Or perhaps you're moving to Brooklyn, getting married, or getting an MBA. The Fool could represent a new medical treatment or a home renovation project.

The Fool tells you it's time to go for it on life's journey. No rules, no plans. Pack light but bring your childlike sense of wonder.

REVERSED FOOL

Fool's errand, false promise, repeating a pattern, an ill-advised choice

When the Fool card is reversed, it can mean the person may think they are doing something new, but really it is the same old pattern and will not offer them any growth. Instead of initiating new energy, they are being foolish.

I read for a client for many years who chased deal after deal, trying one get-rich-quick scheme after another. Each time he came in for a reading, he had a new 'amazing opportunity' to check out, and I always said the same thing. After a few years, he changed it up and instead asked how the cards looked for 'an exciting new business venture with major potential.'

He withheld details that would have revealed it was yet another get-rich-quick scheme. It didn't matter because he got the Fool card reversed again, so I knew he was up to his same tricks.

There can be some trickster energy when the Fool card is reversed and things may not be as they seem. Maybe the person is stuck in an abusive relationship cycle, but erroneously thinks it will be different this time. Or maybe they are starting yet another self-help technique instead of increasing their self love. There is potential for self-delusion when the Fool card is reversed.

The Fool card reversed can mean you're being made a fool of. Someone may be offering you false gold. Look at the surrounding cards to determine the nature of the foolishness and whether it is self-deception or if you're being conned.

When the Fool card is reversed, it can signify the avoidance of a new beginning. There may be an unwillingness to take a risk or risking too much on a poor bet. I've seen it a few times where a client knows they need to make a major change, such as ending a relationship or starting a new career, yet they are scared to make the change.

ACTIVATING THE FOOL

Whenever I sit down, my dog runs and finds his green ball and brings it to me, hoping I'll throw it for him. Sometimes I do and sometimes I don't, but he never gives up. He puts the ball in my hand and waits in joyful anticipation. The possibility of me throwing the ball is enough for him. He would probably feel like an idiot if he were a human, but he's so earnest that I can't help but throw the ball for him.

The fear of looking stupid can stop us from trying something new. The Fool enjoys people laughing at them. Their lack of pride and humor are their greatest sources of strength.

Is there something you would like to go for but you're afraid of making a fool out of yourself?

1-7 Foundational Lessons

THE FIRST SEVEN cards of the major arcana are about both awakening and building a sound foundation. You can see them as the developmental stages you go through from conception to early adulthood.

The Magician can represent conception. The High Priestess can represent your time in utero, and the Empress represents the mother archetype with the Emperor representing the father archetype and socialization.

Once you've figured out those relationships, you enter society and learn from the institutions of education, religion or corporations represented by the Hierophant who grants you a sense of how the world works and your place in it.

After you graduate, you're ready to meet and love another person. Learning how to relate is represented by the Lovers card. Then, with the foundation of love, you build your home, community, maybe start a family, and set out in your Chariot to seek your fame and fortune.

An entire multitude of things can go wrong at any stage of human development. It's possible to be 65 years old and to be stuck back at conception, believing you were unwanted or unwelcome. You can have mother or father issues blocking you from progressing. Or you can be traumatized by school or confused by religion and never really get past it.

When these first seven tarot cards show up, it can help illuminate where you may be stuck in a particular area of your development and in your life.

1. Magician

Element: Air

Manifesting, alchemy, making stuff happen, the field of all possibilities

The Magician stands with their right arm pointed toward the sky while holding a double pointed wand, invoking both the spiritual and the physical world. They point their left finger down toward the earth.

The Magician reaches for the stars and brings them down to earth. They are a channel for manifestation. The infinity symbol crowns them, showing that they are in touch with the limitless potential of the Universe.

Laid on the table before the Magician are the four suits: a pentacle, a cup, a sword, and a wand. The Magician has mastered the tools and has command of them. White lilies and red roses surround them. The white symbolizes purity, idealism, spirituality while the rose signifies passion and desire.

The Magician is the first major arcana card and the beginning of the tarot journey. This is when you realize it's your life and you're free to choose, no matter what your circumstances may be.

The Magician card shows an understanding of the field of all possibilities and how we collapse the field based on our belief systems. This is when we see patterns and realize we have the power to choose our response.

The Magician is an alchemist and an agent of transformation. The energies evoked by an awakening process can be powerful and disruptive.

Alchemists use a container called a crucible to purify and transform substances. The crucible contains the energies and allows them to change. The key to awakening is to stay in the crucible as the pressure builds and allow yourself to be transformed.

It's challenging to not escape, and it's easy to become confused by the overlay of emotional currents. Emotions signal an awakening and detoxing what longer serves you. What we can transform is how our experience is organized and reconfigure the networks holding our wounds.

The Magician helps us to transmute the rust and tin of lack, control, and sacrifice into the gold of knowing you have unlimited potential. When you activate this transformation, you become the artist of your new world.

REVERSED MAGICIAN

Blocked, false magic, frustrated, struggle, misdirected energy, manipulation

When the Magician is reversed, you may feel like your life is just happening to you and you have no choice. Maybe you feel like a victim but haven't realized the frequencies attracting your problematic situations are being generated by you.

Or maybe you're struggling and unknowingly wasting your power by trying to control others.

The Magician card reversed can also show a lack of direction or an unwillingness to get into the driver's seat of your life. This can come from a fear of making a mistake or not wanting to take responsibility for outcomes in your life.

You may not know what you want, or you may feel timid or unwilling to take the risk of going for what you want.

Activating the Magician

As you awaken, everything that is not you will burn off. This purification process can be challenging to navigate.

You may find that you suddenly can't stand any of your playlists. Your friends may change, or you may realize you're better suited for a different line of work.

Try to stay in your crucible and allow yourself to be transformed.

What would you like to transform in your life?

2. High Priestess

Element: Water

Feminine wisdom, initiation, esoteric wisdom, intuition, inner voice

The High Priestess is the real deal. They know what's up, and they see Right. Through. You. Many can't handle or understand this energy until they are at least 30, often older. Sometimes it takes becoming a parent or another intense life event before the High Priestess allows you through the gates.

The High Priestess sits at an entrance between two pillars, representing duality of positive/negative, the pillars of Kabbalah, masculine/feminine, and dark/light.

One pillar is black with the letter B (Boaz, meaning 'in his strength') and the other is white with the letter J (Jachin, meaning 'he will establish'). Acceptance of the dualistic nature of life is required to enter this sacred space.

The High Priestess's crown symbolizes the connection with Isis, the Egyptian goddess of wisdom, mother, and fertility. On their lap, they hold a scroll representing sacred and secret esoteric wisdom such as Akashic records or the Torah. The moon at their feet is also sacred to the goddess and symbolizes contemplative reflection.

Behind the priestess is the Veil of Unknowing covered with pomegranates, hiding the mystery of existence and alluding to the myth of Persephone and the wisdom gained during her six months in the underworld.

After the conception of the Magician, comes the embodiment of consciousness. The High Priestess is the entrance to the womb door and to the matrix of the third-dimensional reality. The High Priestess can lift the Veil of Unknowing and allow you to peek at the truth of your existence, but only if you can handle it.

The High Priestess is a card of the divine feminine, sacred knowledge, esoteric wisdom, mystery, stillness and passivity. They represent the feminine aspects of consciousness and sacred knowledge and the subconscious mind.

The High Priestess may tell you to spend more time in reflection or meditation. Or maybe they are reminding you to trust your inner knowing.

In the dominant culture of the United States, we are praised and rewarded for approaching life with goals, achievement, and production. The High Priestess sadly shakes their head. When will they learn? And we desperately want to learn, but the High Priestess turns many seekers away because they aren't ready.

You can't truly learn the esoteric or magical arts from books and flashcards. It can't be approached intellectually. They must be sensed and felt. Absorbed by moonlight. You must let go of everything that isn't your knowing, that isn't your truth. Be still. And pay attention.

And let's be clear, the gate represented in this card is reminiscent of another "gate" in the female anatomy. A lesser discussed aspect of this card can be about sexuality, boundaries and respect.

We can look to the High Priestess for healing after any sort of abusive situation. The High Priestess tells us we're Right as we are. That our ways of knowing and processing are Right and we need to respect ourselves and our innate wisdom.

Reversed High Priestess

Secrets, misogyny, disconnection with inner truth, disrespect, false spirituality

When the High Priestess is reversed, there can be secrets, disharmony, not listening to intuition, or rejection of feminine aspects of consciousness. They may tell you to unlearn your feminine conditioning.

The person drawing this card reversed may be overly analytical or distrusting of nonlinear, non-scientific experience. They may not connect with their innate knowing.

Some think that living their truth hurts others, so they'll live their lives based on not hurting others and not incurring disapproval. They'll pass up wonderful opportunities in order to keep the peace or because they are afraid of making a mistake.

I read for an older woman who had recently broken her ankle. She drew the High Priestess card reversed. I talked about deferring dreams, always serving others, and the basics of feminine conditioning. She grew sad as she remembered how, as a young girl, she desperately wanted to be a dancer, but didn't want to burden her family with the cost and the transportation to and from practice.

The High Priestess can illuminate unintegrated spirituality, spiritual posturing, or ego-driven seeking. She may also highlight codependency or a lack of sovereignty.

Physically, this card can refer to hormones, fertility, the menstrual cycle, and uterus in particular. It can also show relationship issues with the mother.

ACTIVATING THE HIGH PRIESTESS

Tap into The High Priestess for a mic check on your inner voice. She can help you increase the volume of your intuition.

When was the last time you let your inner voice guide you?

3. EMPRESS

ELEMENT: Earth

Abundance, creativity, motherhood, embodiment, feminine consciousness

Ah, the lovely Empress. After the initiation and potential of the High Priestess, we're ready to create something for Real. The Empress is one hot earth mama. She exudes sensuality and beauty, not to mention love, abundance, creativity, fertility and growth. The Empress is Gaia embodied.

The Empress sits in luxurious comfort, crowned with twelve stars, demonstrating her connection with the mystical realm and the cycles of the natural world.

Lush images of growth and fertility encircle her. A beautiful, lush forest and winding stream surrounds the Empress, signifying her connection with Mother Earth and life itself. Her castle is nature. Wheat grows at her feet, symbolizing nourishment and the association of harvest.

The Empress ensures that growth occurs, and bounty is harvested. She also reminds you that the seeds you sow are in direct relation to the harvest you reap.

Wheat is a symbol of the life cycle - a time to sow, a time to grow and a time to pick the fruits of your labor. The Empress is aware of time and the part it plays in manifesting your desires. It can take time to see the process of your desire unfold into reality.

The waterfall to her left symbolizes motion, emotion, abundance, and the ability of the Empress to open up intuitive resources and for abundance to flow freely. The waterfall is a reminder that with tranquility also comes extreme force. You must be mindful of your capacity to love and create, as well as your ability to hate and destroy.

A cushion features the symbol of Venus, the planet of love, creativity, fertility, beauty, art, pleasure, and grace, the essence of the Empress.

Her robe is decorated with pomegranates, alluding to the Persephone and Demeter myth in which Demeter, who was the goddess of the harvest, lost her daughter to the underworld. There are also pomegranates decorating the veil in the High Priestess card. The Empress has incorporated the esoteric wisdom of the High Priestess and is now embodying it.

This card is the mother lode. She often represents pregnancy and motherhood. Many decks depict the Empress as pregnant and she can convey a message of either a physical pregnancy or a situation pregnant with promise. She represents the creative power of feminine consciousness.

The Empress is the one who will help you learn the guitar, belly dance, figure out how to make Baked Alaskan or how to have multiple orgasms. She can help you gestate and birth your dreams, but through allowing and receiving, not by forcing and doing.

"Trust the natural process," she says. If you are fully invoking the Empress, you probably aren't reading this right now because you're immersed in experiencing life.

Unlike the cool, esoteric and somewhat virginal High Priestess, the Empress is fully embodied. She has recovered from her Catholic upbringing and is comfortable in her sensuality.

The Empress is associated with the creative exploration of life. She encourages us to use our senses to engage with the world.

In a reading, The Empress usually represents an archetype more than an actual person. However, The Empress card can represent an actual person who is helping you learn the lessons the Empress represents.

Reversed Empress

Shame, inability to receive, guilt, rejection of physicality, lack

When the Empress card is reversed, it can feel like the part in the Greek myth of Demeter and Persephone when Demeter is searching and grieving for her lost daughter, Persephone, resulting in crops dying and the season of winter. There can be a lack of growth, stagnation, or blocked creativity.

Maybe your project is stuck or feeling uninspired. Maybe you lack strong boundaries and are being taken advantage of.

The Empress could represent feelings of insecurity and shame. Maybe you don't love your body and struggle with being embodied. Or maybe you can't allow yourself to enjoy or receive pleasure.

Depending on how you were raised, you may have been encouraged to be nice, accommodating, and submissive. It's embedded in every Disney princess movie, so it's hard to escape the messages. It's getting better, but females in particular are often encouraged to put others first, be supportive, and look pretty.

At some point, it's not enough to be a cheerleader. Wouldn't it be more fun to be in the action on the field? There's nothing wrong with being in a supportive role, but it will not be sustainable if it hurts you or takes away your right to live your life on your terms.

The other response to the culturally dominant perception of masculine consciousness being superior to the feminine, is to negate these feminine aspects of consciousness. Sadly, many think if they want to be competitive, successful, or powerful, they can only do so by rejecting the feminine and adopting more masculine values and approaches.

It doesn't have to be a problem, but anything that requires energy to force, reject or suppress can demand attention later in order to regain balance.

When the Empress is reversed, it could signal a lack of resources. It can feel like there's not enough love, money or time. There could be distrust, overindulgence, or an imbalance with sensuality.

The mother represented by the Empress card reversed is wounded in her feminine consciousness, likely by her own relationship with her mother or simply from internalized religious and cultural messages described above.

As a result, she may be alienated from her body, her creativity, and from her natural instincts. The overcompensation could be patterns of control, sacrifice, and dismissal of feminine aspects of consciousness.

ACTIVATING THE EMPRESS

Our bodies hold the key to reclaiming the truth of who we are. They are the best tool we have to reclaim our wild nature. Trusting your body is the first step to claiming responsibility for your health and wellbeing.

Are there any areas of your life that could use some pleasure or sensuality?

4. Emperor

Element: Fire

Patriarchy, authority, structure, power, discipline

The Emperor is In Charge. He is the Divine Masculine and the alpha male. You can find him as a CEO, a President, a King, a general, the police, a coach, or a father figure.

The Emperor holds an Ankh scepter in his right hand and a globe, symbolizing domination, in his left. A foot clad in armor pokes out from under his robe. The Emperor is ready for war and willing to use whatever it takes to enforce his agenda.

There are rocky, barren mountains in the background and he sits on a cold, solid stone throne, representing the sterility of regulation and unyielding power. The Emperor can appear harsh and austere, especially compared to the Empress.

He symbolizes the top of the secular hierarchy, the ultimate masculine ego. No one takes the Emperor's parking spot. There is no softness here, no comfort, no apologies, and definitely no milk and cookies.

The dominant color of this card is red which is associated with the planet Mars, a planet of action, war, and anger. You don't want to anger the Emperor, but the Emperor will play fair, (at least when upright), so you will deserve what you get.

We need the Emperor to get stuff done in our lives and to have success, order, control, boundaries, strategy and organization. The Emperor helps you to discipline yourself, not in a punishing way (unless reversed), but in the way of directing your energy productively toward your goals.

The Emperor can represent authority, boundaries, power, success, money, responsibility for others, and laying down the law. The Emperor can imply that it is time to employ strategic and analytic thinking or to take decisive action.

There is not a lot of patience for process, nor a lot of allowance for differing opinions with the Emperor. This is not an open-minded peace and love card. This is a clear, decisive leadership, and productive action card.

While the Empress represents the mother principle, the Emperor represents the father principle and the socialization of the child. The Emperor card signifies the relationship with masculine aspects of consciousness which we learned from our institutions and authority figures.

This card is usually not an actual person, although it can represent the way you experience a specific person or situation. A court card would usually represent the real person. If a person seems to be represented by the Emperor card, it is because the person is activating father or authority issues.

The Emperor is the coach who tells you to suck it up when you're in catcher's gear and it's 90 degrees out, and you become a better player and a better person because of it. The Emperor is a generous, powerful ruler who doesn't mess around and won't tolerate you messing around, either.

Reversed Emperor

Control, dictatorship, impatience, intolerance, abuse of power

The problem is when we internalize the Emperor and then tyrannize ourselves with an imbalance of masculine energy. Because reversed, the Emperor is scary. This archetype can manifest as a sociopath, a psychopath, a narcissist, or a dictator. He can be a big time control freak.

As a father, he can appear selfish, abusive, excessively authoritarian, and possibly damaging to the child. He may not control his anger and may force his agenda on the child instead of allowing the child to develop naturally on their own terms.

In a relationship, the reversed Emperor archetype may need to control and dominate everyone and everything around them. It can feel like it's all about them. All the time.

The reversed Emperor may feel like he owns you, which justifies the confiscation of your wedding ring for non-compliance, monitoring devices in your car, or eavesdropping on your therapy sessions.

When you catch the reversed Emperor cheating, he'll say that you 'made them have to cheat' on you because he can't admit when he's wrong.

Fun is in short supply when this guy is reversed, although there may be a lot of drama if you like that sort of thing.

The person who is acting like the Emperor reversed is probably overcompensating for deep insecurity, which may be hard to remember when you find the hidden cameras pointed at you in your bedroom.

On a universal level, the Emperor represents the patriarchy. If you've drawn this card reversed, you may recognize in yourself the patterns of behavior those in a subordinate role use to adapt in order to survive the dominant culture.

When the oppression of the Emperor is internalized, there can be traits of blind compliance, lack of initiative, abandonment of self, avoidance of anger, passivity and fear of showing power. These coping behaviors are often reinforced through education, religion, and popular culture.

The Emperor reversed may mean you're not taking decisive action or you need better boundaries. The Emperor reversed may tell you that you need more structure.

Conversely, it can also mean there is too much structure, and it is stultifying and smothering you, such as anorexia, where control around food is out of balance with true nourishment.

People with the negative masculine introject represented by the Emperor may have issues with internal and external authority. There could be issues with weight and appearance. Often there is difficulty with receiving, particularly receiving pleasure, because it requires the surrender of control.

For example, I had a client trying to launch her business who was doing everything right but wasn't getting any sales. In her three-card daily tarot spread, and she kept pulling the Emperor reversed.

When she dug a little deeper, she connected the reversed Emperor with her father, who earned all the money in her family growing up but had been abusive. The belief she had from childhood was: having money meant she had to either let herself be bullied like her mother, or else she had to be abusive like her father.

She was in a pickle for sure which is why she wasn't making any money. Once she realized the dynamics at play, she could integrate and relate to a healthy masculine support structure and move forward with her business.

ACTIVATING THE EMPEROR

The Emperor asks you to get chummy with the supportive aspects of masculine consciousness.

How can discipline be your friend?

5. Hierophant

Element: Earth

Higher learning, spiritual wisdom, religious beliefs, convention, institutions

What comes after the absolute summit of human, masculine power and leadership? The need for social structure, institution, and spiritual governance.

As the dominant ego attitudes, symbolized by the Emperor, are no longer expansive enough to contain what is developing in the unconscious, or when the heart is no longer involved in the ego's concerns, then the Emperor's authority dissolves and the ego realizes its limitations and gradually surrenders to a higher power.

The new consciousness is not only conscious, but depends on a higher power. The independent attitude of the Emperor, that believed personal power sufficed to take him toward progress and liberation, is now perceived as insulated and arrogant. With the Hierophant, the ego acknowledges a spiritual authority that transcends ego-hood.

The Hierophant is a religious figure sitting between two pillars of a sacred temple, though this temple differs from the one in which the High Priestess sits.

The Hierophant wears three robes, red, blue and white, and a three-tiered crown, representing the three worlds over which they rule: the conscious, subconscious and superconscious.

In their left hand, they hold the Papal Cross, a triple scepter signifying their religious status. The Hierophant raises their right hand in a religious blessing, with two fingers pointing towards Heaven and two towards Earth.

Before the Hierophant kneel two followers. The Hierophant's task is to pass down spiritual wisdom and initiate the two into the church so they can take up their appointed roles. Red roses represent Venus and passion, while the white lily represents purity and innocence.

The crossed keys at the Hierophant's feet represent the keys to the universe. Crossed represents balance between the conscious and subconscious minds and the unlocking of mysteries, which the Hierophant can teach.

This imagery speaks to a shared group identity and to a rite of passage. The Hierophant represents having achieved a high level of spiritual growth. They represent the search for knowledge and illumination. The search for truth. The Hierophant is a spiritual teacher and leader.

The Hierophant is the masculine counterpart to the High Priestess and is known as the Pope or the Teacher in other decks. Ideally, the Hierophant hears the divine will and transmits it to others without bias.

The Hierophant is associated with the sign of Taurus. Taurus is an Earth sign and pertains to the tangible, material aspects of life. This means the Hierophant represents teachings through school, books, the internet, spiritual study, and classes on the earthly plane.

If you were burned by religion, education or soul-sucking institutions that insisted on compliance and obedience, you may take umbrage with the archetype of the Hierophant. However, we need spiritual teachers and we need social structures in order to understand and manage our individual and collective experiences.

This card can represent marriage, academia, medicine, government or any other tradition or social institution to which we subscribe and look to for definition and security.

Reversed Hierophant

Dogma, guru-ism, convention, compliance, reclaiming truth, sovereignty

When the Hierophant card is reversed, it can represent any system that suppresses and limits the search for spiritual truth.

It could represent a dogmatic religion or a repressive belief system. Or it could represent an old school work environment refusing to evolve with the times that is intolerant of independent thought or initiative.

The Hierophant reversed can represent challenging the status quo, or questioning the beliefs you've been spoon-fed. The most obvious example of the Hierophant reversed is joining a cult, but there are much more subtle systems to which we subscribe but rarely examine, such as our relationship with time.

The Hierophant reversed can signal the exorcism of convention and internalized social norms, including productive actions such as the breaking of rules in order to discover the truth. In this sense, the Hierophant reversed can mean divorce as a path to wholeness and a way of reclaiming true intimacy, versus playing out the socially prescribed roles of husband or wife.

Or, on the end of the spectrum, it can mean getting married or staying married in order to comply with social expectations. For example, a client, who started dating her husband when she was 15, drew the Hierophant card reversed. She was in her 30s with two kids and realized she skipped quite a few developmental stages. She was wondering what she missed by trying to be a "good" daughter and "good" wife.

Raised with strong rules and religious beliefs about how females should act, she received powerful negative messages about sex. But she followed all the rules and did everything "right". She loved her husband, but realized she got married for all the wrong reasons and now she and her husband were trying to grow themselves up from age 15 and it was messy.

The Hierophant reversed can mean you're being overly compliant or overly trusting of authority. It can show you're caring too much about the opinions of others.

Depending on the placement, it can represent bigotry and intolerance, blind faith in dogma, or gullibility. The Hierophant reversed can signify clinging to an institution for self-definition.

The Hierophant card, and also the Hermit card reversed, can show up for those addicted to spiritual seeking, chasing after the latest truth-seeking fad.

ACTIVATING THE HIEROPHANT

A quick look at history will show that what is considered 'true' and 'right' changes every couple decades.

Have you ever looked for truth in the wrong places?

6. Lovers

Element: Air

Love, relationship, deep soul connection, passion, a romantic encounter

The Lovers card depicts a Garden of Eden setting with the serpent, the tree of wisdom, and the fruit that got Adam and Eve booted out of the garden and into the matrix of flesh and sensuality.

The angel portrayed in the Lovers card is Raphael, the angel of air. You'd think Venus, the planet of love and beauty, would rule this card, but it's ruled by Mercury and the sign of Gemini, which is the sign of the twins, representing the duality in relationships. The Lovers card depicts the idea that it is through loving another you can experience more of your connection to divinity.

The Lovers card is the sixth card of the major arcana. Six is the number of community, balance, relationships, and service. After you move through the teachings of the first five major arcana cards, you can discover true love and the higher purpose of relationships.

In order to experience the healthy love represented by the Lovers card, you would have to be embodied (Empress, mother, nurture); have self-control (Emperor, father, socialization); and know your own truth (Hierophant). Sometimes, you may need to go through a separation, divorce, or breakup (Hierophant) in order to liberate yourself from social expectations, heal unhealthy patterns of codependency and learn to love from choice.

Once you've moved through these lessons, and become strong in who you are, then you're ready to learn through being in a relationship with another.

When the Lovers card shows up in a reading, you're opening up to experience more love in connection with another being. It does not have to be romantic. It can represent a pet being adopted, for example, opening the new owner to experiencing unconditional love.

The Lovers card can definitely signify a romantic encounter and often does. When the Lovers card shows up in a reading, there are deeper connections and larger forces at work.

The romantic connection represented by the Lovers card may feel fated or uncannily familiar. You may feel as if you finally met a member of your tribe or a soul mate. You likely have some healing work to do with this person. There is usually a significant past life connection, particularly if the Moon card is also present. The court cards can give more clues about who the beloved is.

Just because someone draws this card, doesn't mean they should jump in bed or into matrimony. It simply means there is a strong connection with potential life lessons. A significant relationship will probably follow as a way for those life lessons to be learned.

Tarot cards don't care about time or details. They don't care if the person is from four years ago, is already married to someone else, or is your therapist.

Drawing this card can feel exciting, especially when you're in the throes of a new romantic encounter. However, the potent love you experience together can function like a floodlight, illuminating your wounds and blocks to intimacy.

When you see this card, it is about a relationship with a bigger purpose. Whether it's upright or reversed will tell you how you're engaging with your 'intimacy workshop.'

REVERSED LOVERS

Unavailable, relationship ending, disharmony, unhealthy relationship, fear of intimacy

The problem is we don't always interpret "loving" relationships as, well, loving. Sometimes the person who gets your goat the most is the one who is giving you the greatest opportunity for awakening.

The Lovers card reversed will show you any relationship that is pushing you to do your healing work. When the Lovers card is reversed, it can mean you haven't gotten your lesson from the relationship.

In these cases, sorting out the relationship holds the key to your awakening. Not necessarily with the person directly, but looking into why they trigger you so much and exploring what needs to be completed and healed.

They are probably shining a light on an area of yourself you're unaware of or would prefer to keep hidden. Maybe they trigger your abandonment wounds, for example. Or they remind you of your older sibling who bullied you.

When you've done your inner healing work, they will automatically fall off like a scab, leaving you available, and stronger, for a new relationship.

The Lovers card may come up reversed about a significant relationship many years in the past, even decades. Often the person thinks they are over it, but the cards (and their life) will show them the truth, since they probably cannot manifest another significant relationship until they have completed the stuck one. The stuck part is usually their role in the relationship's failure.

When the Lovers card is reversed, it can mean you're repeating a pattern or projecting your shadow onto your partner. Maybe you're afraid of losing the relationship and are compromising yourself in order to "keep" them. If you have to change yourself in order to "get" or "keep" a relationship, it's not good for anyone.

Internally, the Lovers card reversed can signal a deficit of self-love. Maybe you're suffering from feelings of low self-esteem or unworthiness and need to work on loving yourself more before you'll be able to love another.

The Lovers card reversed can illuminate the need to control or be controlled in order to maintain the illusion of security. It can signify unhealthy or toxic relationships. Maybe you feel smothered or like your significant other is sucking the life out of you. Maybe your significant other has an addiction, a mental health issue, or is emotionally unavailable.

It's possible you simply lost that loving feeling. Relationships end, but it can be hard to let go of relationships even once they are naturally complete. The Lovers card reversed may tell you to let go and to move on.

ACTIVATING THE LOVERS

When there are difficulties in intimate relationships, it's helpful to look for patterns where you are the common denominator. Maybe the last three people you dated were unavailable. Or maybe your relationships consistently end after 18 months. Perhaps you date people who are needy. Bringing awareness to your patterns and addressing the root cause can grant you new thresholds of intimacy.

What are the patterns in your significant relationships?

7. CHARIOT

ELEMENT: Water

Drive, determination, discipline, engagement, goals, going for it

Now that the Fool has learned how to be in a relationship, they are ready to set out into the world on a quest to find their truth. The Chariot card represents love in action. It's a simple concept but can be hard to practice. It requires discipline, patience, and attention.

The Chariot card is about being who you are and doing what you are meant to do in the world. Success, the Chariot card reminds us, requires courage, willpower, and focus.

The Chariot is the seventh card of the major arcana. Seven is the number of inner growth, spiritual awakening, introspection, wisdom, and intuition. The Chariot is associated with the sign of Cancer which relates to emotions, family, community, and the home.

While the Chariot symbolizes a drive to achieve specific goals, it is also about using goals as a vehicle to reach self-realization. When you listen to your inner promptings, you can hear yourself being called to do certain tasks and can direct your energy and intent. In this way, the Chariot card can be thought of as a quest for your holy grail.

When you undertake your quest, you're living your truth versus chasing a false goal that stems from ego and approval-seeking. Most often, we seek our holy grail through our work. However, your job or how you make money may not be your genuine work. Your genuine work may be your relationship with your child, the land, or your community.

The figure in the Chariot is leaving behind the comfort and security of the village and venturing out into unfamiliar territory. Family forms your first definition of love, but familial love can also limit you.

The home protects the family, which becomes the physical vessel for love, but the Chariot is also about the home within. In this way, the Chariot card represents the individuation process, where you consciously leave the influence of your family in order to realize yourself and determine your own fate.

The charioteer has the stars above their head, indicative of dreams and destiny. The driver's armor symbolizes awareness of dangers involved and the ability to adapt to have protection. It's also reminiscent of the shell of the crab, the symbol of the sign of Cancer.

The black and white sphinxes are key symbols in The Chariot card. The ability to hold these oppositional forces needs to be in balance in order to move forward into fresh territory.

The Chariot card shows the willingness to set off into unfamiliar territory and to bravely face whatever is in front of you.

REVERSED CHARIOT

Misdirected energy, wrong direction, undisciplined, misalignment, lack of purpose

Imagine what would happen if each Sphinx went in a different direction. The chariot would get stuck, go nowhere, or crash. The driver's focus directs the chariot to go where it wants to go.

When the Chariot is reversed, it is possible to be overcome by emotions or to experience a lack of emotional awareness. This can manifest as blaming, self-deception, and can be self-destructive.

The Chariot reversed can show fear, lack of focus, lack of purpose, indolence, or stubbornness. You may feel stuck or there could be a lack of responsibility, accompanied by an excess of excuses.

You may do the right thing, but for the wrong reasons. Maybe the business or career idea the Chariot represents stems from attachment instead of inspiration. Maybe you're lacking motivation. Or maybe you are dragging your family system behind your chariot.

One client drew this card reversed because he wanted to forge his own path but was stuck working in the family business. He was raised as the 'golden child' in his family and the weight of their expectations was paralyzing him.

None of his job or entrepreneurial prospects looked good because they were stemming from a desire to escape the family business coupled with his identity staked on being successful.

He had been the captain and quarterback of his high school football team, and married the most popular cheerleader, yet he couldn't actualize his true potential as an adult. He couldn't allow himself to fail and he couldn't risk listening to the promptings of his inner voice.

Interestingly, his two sisters who were raised as "chopped liver" compared to his "golden child" assignment were less burdened by heavy expectations and were significantly more successful than him.

I encouraged him to quietly try something to which he felt deeply drawn with no expectation of success or compensation. To let himself fail, flounder, struggle and to be messy and foolish. Without an audience or the pressure of needing to succeed, he realized he liked law, and even though he had to start from scratch, the cards looked promising because it was more aligned with who he was.

ACTIVATING THE CHARIOT

The Chariot can't go anywhere without clear direction. Many of us have been conditioned to please, to accommodate, and to help. It can feel uncomfortable to put your needs first.

When someone asks you to help, try pausing, taking a breath, and checking in with yourself to evaluate what you really want.

You can say, "Let me see if that will work for me." If it doesn't feel good for you, simply say, "That won't work for me." This puts you back in the driver's seat of your life.

In what areas of your life can you be more in the driver's seat?

8-14 Transformation & Evolution

THE FOOL now has a sound foundation and is successfully launched. The seven cards in the next set, from Strength through Temperance, help the Fool learn how to develop and transform through awareness of physicality, adversity, and the impact of actions on others.

The Strength card teaches you how to access your inner fortitude while the Hermit urges you to soul search. After you've defined truth for yourself through the Hermit, you're ready to enter the marketplace and get your butt kicked by the slings and arrows of fortune represented by the Wheel of Fortune.

Once you've released the attachment to the illusion of success and you're willing to transcend the Wheel altogether, then it's time to learn the ultimate wisdom of Justice.

After Justice has schooled you, The Hanged Man forces a time out to integrate the karmic lessons Justice meted out, including a mini existential crisis where your world may feel temporarily suspended in order to reassess.

The Death card follows the Hanged Man to clear out unsupportive aspects of your identity. After all this fun, it's time to kick back with Temperance and patiently trust the process while you reset.

8. Strength

Element: Fire

Courage, fortitude, self-determination, self-control, confidence

The Strength card depicts a figure effortlessly opening the mouth of a lion. The infinity symbol on the Strength card represents the infinite potential available when your mental, physical, emotional and spiritual bodies are aligned.

There is a cheery, hopeful yellow background with a blue mountain representing the challenges overcome to achieve this harmonious state. The serene figure has tamed the lion. Their strength allows them to put their hands near the mouth of a lion without being hurt.

The angelic character wears a white robe representing purity and innocence, but not naivety. Red roses on their robe and in their hair represent awareness, control, and acceptance of their instinctual nature.

Often people want to skip Strength's sometimes uncomfortable lessons and go straight to the wisdom seeking of the Hermit card. This rarely works because without doing the work of reclaiming and balancing the wild and wounded parts of themselves, they only find other people's truth.

What happens if there are no rules? No cages?

The lion represents the wild part of us. It symbolizes our primitive survival instincts, passion, and base desires, such as lust, greed, and hunger. In the Strength card, the wildness of the lion is cooperative, not caged and not controlled. The lion tames itself in order to be touched by the angelic figure who has no fear. So too our wildness and primitive instincts need to be loved and accepted.

In the Thoth deck, this card is called Lust, and it often correlates with sex and sexual experiences because it symbolizes an expanded definition of strength that incorporates our animal nature.

The Strength card asks you to reclaim yourself. All of yourself. Especially your body. It wants us to extricate our bodies from social programming and rigid containers of the Emperor and Hierophant.

What happens when you don't control your intake of food? When you don't restrict your sexual expression? When you don't deny, or repress, or restrain your voice?

The Strength card reminds us that our appetites and desires are natural and right. Getting to know the hidden and vulnerable parts of you helps you find strength. Once you love and accept all parts of yourself, it deepens your compassion for everyone.

The Strength card represents the effortless power you embody when you integrate all parts of yourself, especially the parts that have been suppressed. It tells us to engage with our desires. To own it.

The Strength card shows you're in alignment with your life force. If you've drawn this card, you may feel a deep sense of power and courage to overcome obstacles. Or maybe you are experiencing wonderful sex. You may exude confidence, and you'll probably be successful in your undertaking because you have the strength to make it happen.

REVERSED STRENGTH

Weakness, shame, pride, misdirected sexual energy, lack of self-discipline

When the Strength card is reversed, the animal part of your brain is in charge, and you may be operating from fear. When we don't accept the wild part of ourselves, the lion may take over, lashing out, ripping your life to shreds. Or worse, the lion is put in a cage, perhaps sedated with medicine to keep it calm and docile while the juiciest parts of ourselves slowly wither away.

Fear can show up in a lot of ways. There may be self-destructive behaviors and a lack of willpower or self-control. Conversely, the response to fear may be too much control, or allowing yourself to be controlled by others.

This card often surfaces reversed with people who have codependent tendencies where they confuse a person or situation such as a job as the source of their strength. Instead of trying to control someone else or a part of yourself that you don't like, are afraid of, or think is ugly, let it be. Allow it to inform you. Engage with it. It's there for a reason. You're right as you are. True strength comes from total acceptance of your experience.

When reversed, the Strength card may show a justification of actions that are not in integrity or are cowardly. You may need to have that tough conversation, set a boundary, or pay your parking tickets.

I read for a client whose husband told her that the problem in their marriage was that she was "disobedient". He was deeply insecure and fearful which he mitigated by controlling those around him. In order to punish her and train her to be a "good", compliant wife, he confiscated and hid her wedding ring for over a decade.

In a way his punishment worked. She realized she didn't need someone to control her in order to feel secure. Her lesson was: Don't let anyone put you in a cage. Ever. She left the marriage soon after this realization.

But the worst cages are the ones that we put ourselves in. As bad as he was, she was worse to herself inside. When you put yourself in a prison of control, your authentic experience becomes suppressed.

Maybe you're feeling weak inside, unable to exert your power. Or maybe you have relationships where you're codependent or feel less-than.

Maybe you have a family member you can't stand up to. Without inner strength, it is easy to be taken over by someone else or to succumb to bad habits.

There are often sexual themes rumbling around with the Strength card representing an inability to receive pleasure and deep guilt and shame about sexuality. Maybe you're using sex to avoid intimacy. Or maybe you've repressed your natural urges so much you can't experience an orgasm. Culture and religion can give mixed messages about sexuality that often have to be worked through in order to reclaim your sexuality.

When all aspects of the self aren't operating in coherence, then unresolved issues can come out sideways and wreak havoc in our lives and relationships.

I read tarot at a party where a married, male guest drew the Strength card reversed next to the Queen of Wands reversed, representing a female guest at the party.

Later that night, the real life Queen of Wands reversed started a dance line while waving her underwear over her head in the air in a distorted nod to the infinity symbol on the Strength card. Sure enough, he had sex with her that night.

The man was rigidly rational, emotionally detached, religious, with a lot of unresolved anger toward women. He used his mental body to suppress his physical and emotional bodies instead of balancing his desire, beliefs, and emotions, as illustrated in the upright Strength card.

Another common interpretation of the Strength card reversed is overcompensation to give the false appearance of strength. This could look like arrogance or superiority to mask deep feelings if inferiority. Maybe your natural confidence is blocked or inhibited, possibly because of a lack of self-love. Maybe you're forcing something from your ego instead of from a deeper, more true source.

True strength requires your willingness to embrace the potency you're meant to wield. And to recognize, but not dwell, on how we lost it in the first place so we don't let it happen again.

ACTIVATING STRENGTH

Reclaiming your wild nature is the key to experiencing your strength. Your wildness may need to be broken out of the prison of expectations and limitations or it may come flying out at you out of nowhere.

Your job is to accept and love all parts of yourself no matter how ugly or scary. Then, and only then, can you live authentically from your own center.

What are some ways you can reclaim your wildness?

9. THE HERMIT

ELEMENT: Earth

Introspection, self-reflection, awareness, solitude, wisdom, truth seeker

The Hermit is the wise elder of tarot. They stand atop a snowy mountain with a wizard's staff in one hand and a lantern in the other. The Hermit is the matured version of the Magician. They earned their golden staff through many trials, and the light from the lantern illuminates the path.

While the Hermit card is dark and gray, it isn't gloomy and hopeless. The Hermit looks to the light. They have reached the peak of the mountain, symbolizing a high state of consciousness.

The light in the Hermit card comes from the lantern, which represents vigilance and truth-seeking in the cold and dark hours of life. The six-pointed light shining from the Hermit's lantern represents the conjunction between two triangles (heaven and earth), and the divine light within each of us.

The Hermit's absence of color represents a withdrawal from external distraction to concentrate on the divine light within. The snow represents the crystallization and purity of thought and the absence of emotion, which can distract us from our truth.

The Hermit card contains a nod to Diogenes, the Greek philosopher who went through the marketplace with a lantern looking for an "honest man".

The Hermit card is the only major arcana card set in winter, representing age and wisdom. The Hermit embodies the quest for enlightenment through self-reflection. This card represents soul-searching and encourages you to acknowledge your deepest feelings and needs.

The Hermit retreats from the external noises of the world in order to connect with their own internal divine light. Only then can they clearly hear and understand the correct direction their life should take.

When the Hermit shows up in a reading, it can represent a time of deep self-reflection. The Hermit is the seeker of inner truth. This card represents a time of solitude, withdrawal, and retreat from distractions. It does not mean loneliness.

Many nod in recognition when they draw the Hermit card. There may be a sense of pulling back and assessing your life and your choices. Often you're at a pivotal point in your life and need to make a choice. When you can shut out all the noise of daily existence and tune into your inner guidance, you can hear the answers you need.

You may have to avoid social media or certain relationships in order to hear your truth. Maybe you're sleeping more or staying up into the wee hours reading poetry. Maybe you've gone on a formal retreat or you've isolated yourself in a cabin in the woods. Perhaps you wish you could be in the woods, but instead you hole up in your favorite cafe with noise-canceling headphones.

Whatever this withdrawal means, you're giving yourself some time and space to ponder what is true and what the next steps are on your path.

Reversed Hermit

Avoidance of truth, spiritual materialism, isolation, looking for truth in the wrong places

When the Hermit card is reversed, it can remind you to listen to your own truth. The Hermit card reversed may tell you to make time for self-reflection. Conversely, it can mean you're wasting too much time navel-gazing.

Often, the Hermit card is drawn reversed when the quest for truth has been outsourced to a guru, a religion, or to another authority rather than determined for yourself.

I remember the meaning of this card reversed by thinking of the joke about a drunk person searching for their lost keys under the streetlight despite losing the keys in the park because the light was better under the streetlight.

Like the Hierophant card reversed, there may be blind obedience or unexamined beliefs based on family systems or the need for social approval. There is also the potential for spiritual materialism or over-identification with spirituality.

The Hermit card reversed can represent feelings of loneliness, isolation and disconnection. It can mean discomfort or avoidance of social interaction.

Activating the Hermit

The Hermit reminds you to quiet the noise and reconnect with your inner voice and wisdom.

How can you be your own authority?

10. WHEEL OF FORTUNE

ELEMENTS: All

Luck, impermanence, the "slings and arrows" of fortune, this too shall pass, resiliency

The Wheel of Fortune card is the tenth card in the major arcana. The numerology of ten represents the completion of a cycle and also the beginning of a new one.

After retreating to the mountaintop with the Hermit to understand the deep truths of the universe, it is time to re-enter the marketplace, but with an enlightened understanding about how the world wags and what wags it.

Once you've seen the world from the vantage point of the Hermit, the way you define success is changed. You're no longer willing to waste your time on facades and fool's errands.

The Wheel of Fortune card features a demon, reminding you how easy it is to get caught up in greed, ambition, and attachment. Some interpretations consider the demon to be Anubis, the Egyptian god responsible for helping souls cross over after death and to be reborn, continuing the cycle of life.

The message of this card is that success is fleeting. What goes up must come down and then will go up and down again. When you draw this card, it can mean you're learning the lesson of defining success at a higher level.

When upright, the Wheel of Fortune means good luck and fortune are on your side. It portends a fortunate outcome or could represent the success you're already experiencing. Maybe you just landed a large account, received a promotion, or perhaps you're experiencing great popularity.

Just don't get too cocky. The lesson here is everything changes, so make the most of this turn of the wheel.

REVERSED WHEEL OF FORTUNE

Misfortune, self-sabotage, facade of success, failure, loss

The Wheel of Fortune reversed can mean you're down on your luck. Maybe you've been kicked around by fortune and wonder if you'll ever catch a break.

It could signal that you're out of balance in your pursuit of success. It could remind you to take time to smell the roses. Or to reassess your definition of what makes up a life well lived.

Maybe you've become a workaholic or ruthlessly trample others in your haste to get to the top. Perhaps you've become tipsy with the pursuit of power, prestige, and privilege. Maybe you've got your entire identity pinned to your status and external accomplishments and it's time for a correction.

True growth is rarely comfortable. We each have a certain set point of how much success, abundance, and intimacy we can handle. Even though you may consciously want more of these things, your pain body remembers the last time you were successful but ended up hurt and tries to protect you by convincing you to maintain the status quo. Status quo seems safer because it feels familiar.

Your pain body uses fear and control to block you from experiencing what you most desire. What often happens is you subconsciously sabotage your success in order to stay at your set point. For example, maybe you just aced your exams, but then you come home and get into a fight with your roommate about leaving the cupboards open. Or you have a successful job interview and then you get a parking ticket.

My hometown of Excelsior, Minnesota wasn't impressed with the Rolling Stones when they played at a nearly empty Big Reggie's Danceland in 1964 as part of their fledgling United States tour. The lead singer, Mick Jagger ran into Jim 'Mr. Jimmy' Hutmaker the day after their performance while waiting in line at the local drugstore. Jim wanted a cherry coke, but they were out of cherry syrup, "You can't always get what you want," he said to Jagger. Jagger likely considered that moment a low turn on his Wheel of Fortune, but he obviously kept going despite what a small town in Minnesota thought of his band.

The way to increase your set point is to consciously integrate your new level of success. You can do this by taking time to pause, breathe and feel your body after you've experienced more success, intimacy or abundance. Don't speed, don't get drunk, don't call your ex, don't watch infomercials, don't quit your job. Just sit with the heightened energy and get used to it, so it becomes the new set point.

Depending on how much success and growth you just experienced, it may take longer to get used to the newly heightened vibration of you. Noticing your body and breath can help you hang on to your fresh territory.

ACTIVATING WHEEL OF FORTUNE

If you study the biographies of successful people, you'll notice that they have a few things in common. Most of them overcame major internal or external adversity. The majority experienced some sort of wake-up call from ruination such as divorce, illness, or bankruptcy. They all stuck to their inner truth despite what the world thought of them. And they just kept plugging away, doing what they felt was the right thing for them to be doing. The trappings of success came as a byproduct of heeding their calling.

What is calling you?

11. JUSTICE

ELEMENT: Air

Fairness, legal matters, integrity, universal law, conscience

The key with this card is that the figure representing Justice is not blind. Justice has their eyes wide open and sees clearly what is in front of them.

Justice wears red like the Emperor and the Hierophant, who are also about socialization and systems to help humans know the right way to act toward each other.

The Emperor is about human-made laws and the Hierophant card is about institutional, religious, or social laws. The Justice card is bigger than both of them, incorporating universal law.

In their right hand is a double-sided and upright sword. This sword has the power to cut straight to the truth. And off with your head if you deserve it.

In their left hand is a scale with which they can weigh the stories to find the truth. The scales are also a nod to the astrological sign of Libra, a sign known to strive for balance, sometimes at substantial cost to themselves.

The Justice card is number 11 which is a balanced number. In numerology, the number 11 is considered a master number and symbolizes a search for spirituality. 11 is ultimately reduced to the number two (1 + 1), which further symbolizes balance, harmony and diplomacy.

The character on the Justice card sits between two pillars, reminiscent of the High Priestess and the Hierophant. Like the High Priestess, there is a veil behind them.

The Justice card's meaning is easy to remember because it's simply about Justice. The Justice card isn't concerned with human-made laws. Justice is concerned with universal laws and with karma. The Justice card says, "Sorry, the laws of karma apply here. You reap what you sow."

The Justice card comes after the Wheel of Fortune has slapped you in the face with life cycles, mortality and the whims of fame and fortune. The Justice card tells you to pay attention, learn the lesson and take responsibility for your experience.

Often, when the "right" thing happens in a legal proceeding, it still doesn't feel fair or right. When a situation doesn't feel good, something is unresolved. The unresolved aspect may be energetic, heart based, or karmic, and reparations still need to be made.

This card often represents legal cases, insurance claims, divorce, or work situations. It can represent family dynamics where there is favoritism or an imbalance of power. It's less common, but the Justice card can represent a person who works with the law in some capacity or has the potential for restorative authority.

I've seen the Justice card show up when a parent inquires about a child. It can mean the child is concerned with right and wrong and will often become disproportionately upset with even a whiff of unfairness. Usually this is because they are carrying some karma from a past life, often with another family member or they've incarnated to heal some injustice in the family lineage.

Justice can signal a personal process of balancing, such as work and family, or taking stock of what is truly worthy of your time and energy.

If Justice is upright, it usually foretells a favorable outcome as long as you're in integrity.

REVERSED JUSTICE

Unfairness, unresolved, injustice, favoritism, oppression, wrongdoing

When the Justice card is reversed, it simply means injustice. It can represent a legal proceeding that will not resolve in your favor. It can also mean unfair judgements toward you such as prejudice or unfair actions such as stealing.

Maybe you're blaming others and clinging to victimhood instead of taking responsibility for your role in an outcome and learning from it.

One client came in for a consultation after getting a DUI. She was a single mom and couldn't afford to lose her license. She had been out at a restaurant and had a couple drinks. Her intuition told her not to drive. Her boyfriend told her not to drive. Yet she drove, and she forgot to turn her lights on and got pulled over. She was over the legal blood alcohol limit.

She pulled the Justice card reversed because she broke the law and was in the wrong. She hoped the court would make an exception to the law because she wouldn't be able to work without her license.

The Justice card reversed can also signify an internal imbalance, such as trying to keep the peace at the cost of your authenticity. Or being taken advantage of because you're not standing up for yourself.

ACTIVATING JUSTICE

There is a big difference between being nice and being kind. Being nice means you're sacrificing your needs and your authenticity for the perceived benefit of another. At its root are deep feelings of inadequacy. Nice people will avoid conflict by placating others because they can't stand to have anyone be upset with them.

Being kind stems from confidence and clarity about who you are. Kind people operate from a firm foundation of self-esteem and respect themselves as well as others. In order to be kind, you are assertive, set healthy boundaries, and manage conflict constructively. Kind people take responsibility for their own self-care. They're generous, but don't get caught up in a user-pleaser type of relationship.

How can you become less nice and more kind?

12. HANGED MAN

ELEMENT: **Water**

Suspension, time out, contemplation, reparations, re-parenting yourself

Despite hanging upside down by one foot, this character doesn't look like they are suffering too much. Instead, with the halo around their head, it looks like they are learning from their stuck position. The branch from which they're suspended has leaves growing, signifying a period of growth despite inaction.

After you leave the carnival ride of the Wheel of Fortune behind, Justice reminds you there are much bigger laws at play. The Hanged Man gives you the time and altered vantage point to ponder these lessons and apply them to your life.

The Hanged Man comes after the Justice card as punishment for the broken universal laws. The goal of the punishment represented by the Hanged Man is to clear out karma, but not through torture and suffering. It's accomplished through contemplation and a different view of the situation.

The Hanged Man is learning a valuable lesson through surrender. Justice has tied the knots on their feet and hands, and Justice will untie them when the lesson is learned.

This card can show up when you need to retreat from life. The Shelter in Place orders during the 2020 pandemic exemplifies this card. It wrenched most of us out of our habitual zombie modes of the materialistic grind and running from one activity after another. It forced us to be at home and to cook our own food and to face any truths we had successfully distracted ourselves from through being so busy.

Maybe you're frustrated because you can't seem to change a particular situation. The Hanged Man is showing you that you're stuck for a reason with a bigger purpose for the stuck-ness, like the cocoon stage of the butterfly. Try looking at your situation from a different viewpoint, or see if there is something you need to learn in order to move on.

REVERSED HANGED MAN

Forcing, pushing, stuck, blocked, release

When the Hanged Man card is reversed, it can mean a stuck situation is now moving, but more often it signifies that you're not getting the lesson. Either you're avoiding or else stubbornly forcing a stuck situation into some resolution.

Since the Hanged Man comes after the Justice card, it can mean you're not taking responsibility for a situation in your life. One man kept drawing this card reversed because he never took the time to process why he got fired from his last job before jumping into the next job and repeating the pattern.

Being stuck like the Hanged Man can feel as if you're banging your head against a wall. You keep trying and trying but nothing works. This card tells you to just give up. What you're doing isn't working, so just back off, chill out, and try a different approach.

Or, the Hanged Man reversed can mean you are stuck and feel helpless or hopeless. As a result, you're not taking the steps to release yourself from your suffering.

The Hanged Man reversed can mean you're not surrendering and trusting the process to unfold. Or you're too caught up in your situation and you can't get any perspective. Sometimes there can be avoidance through false surrender and not enough culpability and decisive action.

Many people unconsciously defend themselves through the misapplication of spiritual principles. Instead of having a tough conversation with someone they love, for example, they may bless, encase in white light, or burn papers. Or instead of experiencing their emotions, they try to override them with meditation or yoga pose them away.

The problem with these spiritual approaches is they are like putting frosting over garbage. The root problem never gets addressed constructively. This approach is a creative form of avoidance and the person who employs it can "enjoy" feeling holy and even martyred.

I had a client who was going through a divorce. She had been hyper-functional in the marriage and was the main breadwinner. Her husband was drinking, addicted to porn, and not contributing to the household. During the divorce process, her family intervened because she wasn't listening to her lawyer. She disagreed with her lawyer's advice because she felt like her lawyer wasn't applying spiritual principles. She didn't want to be greedy or mean, she just wanted to rise above it all.

"It's just money and stuff. I'm very Zen about the whole thing," she said. And she especially didn't want to fight with her spouse. She pulled the Justice and Hanged Man cards, both reversed, but her Queen of Swords lawyer was upright.

It was a tough conversation, but eventually she understood that fighting for what was fair was the most loving action she could take for everyone involved. She allowed the law and her lawyer to support and guide her, since her inner guidance system was so damaged.

By staying committed to the right thing happening, even though it was uncomfortable, she healed the old patterns of how she related to men. She'd never fought for herself before, and if she hadn't fought for her rights during the divorce process, she would have repeated the pattern.

Activating Hanged Man

Real transformation requires both action and inaction. There will be parts of the process you can control and parts you can't. The key is to take full responsibility for what you can control and then allow life to inform you what the next steps are.

Where in your life are you stuck or feeling frustrated? How can you see the situation from a different point of view?

13. DEATH

ELEMENT: **Water**

Transition, loss, letting go, release, transformation

In older tarot decks, the Hanged Man was hung by his neck as the punishment meted out by Justice. Symbolically, the Death card follows the Hanged Man because after the period of intense reflection represented by the Hanged Man, you realize that it's time to shed all the outgrown ways of life.

In a reading, the Death card rarely means physical death, and instead signifies the transition of leaving an old life behind. The Death card can scare people. It's wise to be cautious interpreting the Death card unless it is in a position representing the past where someone has already died and the person for whom you're reading is trying to process the loss. A physical death is a "transition" and it is safest to adopt this approach.

Near-death experiences can also trigger this card. One client had a terrible car accident and nearly died. They pronounced her dead at the scene and she floated above her body while the paramedics worked on her. She heard voices tell her it wasn't her time yet, and that she still had work to do. Her physical recovery was hard, but her near death experience functioned like a total life reset and she was no longer willing to waste her time and energy on things that didn't matter.

The Death card isn't an easy life lesson, but it's best not to fight it or try to avoid it because it just draws out the suffering. Death will mow down anything not serving your highest good. The more attached you are to your identity and to your stories, the harder it may be to go through this inevitable process.

In tarot consultations, the Death card appears with surprising frequency because people often seek a tarot reading for guidance amid major life change, such as shedding an old identity, a job change, or ending a relationship.

The change doesn't have to be unwanted. It can show up when someone has gender affirming surgery, moves, gets happily married, or has a baby. The Death card can also signify a little death such as your child heading off to kindergarten. It can reflect the completion of a creative project.

It may represent leaving childhood behind when you move out of your childhood home and become an adult. On the other side of the life cycle, it can signify redefining yourself as a parent when your child moves out of your home.

A lot of "deaths" don't register for people or they think since so much time has passed that they're over it. Upright or reversed will tell you if they're in it or whether the grieving process is stuck.

REVERSED DEATH

Resistance to change, stagnation, not letting go, fear of loss, repeating negative patterns

The Death card reversed can mean an inevitable change needs to happen, but is being ignored or avoided. Instead of making an inevitable change, no matter how uncomfortable, you drag it out, creating even more suffering.

This could be like a relationship you know is over, but you keep hanging on because you're afraid of being alone. Or it could represent a job you know you need to quit, but you can't quite pull the trigger on because you fear what will happen next.

The Death card reversed could mean you're emerging from a period of feeling dead or recovering from a major surgery or illness. Or maybe you're currently half-dead because you're staying stuck and suffocating your life force with your unwillingness to change.

Aversion to completion is common with the Death card reversed. When you don't complete an experience, it can stay stuck and become "bookmarked," waiting for you to complete it and hijacking your vitality and your future in the meantime.

It's important to be as present as possible with all endings. Staying comfortable means staying the same. Life is always pushing you to grow and heal, and it is much easier to surrender than it is to fight it and remain "comfortable."

We often have a fixed mental projection of what we think we're losing, such as a relationship you've had for a long time. You think if you let it go it would be a terrible loss, but you're basing the fear of the loss on the habitual mental projection which may have no bearing on the reality of the relationship in the present time.

In present time, the relationship may be dead, unhealthy, no longer a fit, or not nourishing both parties. Or, if you see the dynamic, you may be attached to keeping the connection, even if you know the dynamic isn't good for you because you may use the relationship as an external reference point you check yourself against in order to feel more stable.

We base the fear of loss on the erroneous belief we are separate from source, and as a result, we think we're finite. You forget you're a part of everything, everything is part of you, and that you are an infinite, indestructible consciousness.

When you're stuck in the illusion of separateness, you believe it's possible to lose something, and the tendency is to hang on to what you think you have because you're afraid of losing the thing you don't even really want anymore. The fear of loss can limit you from moving toward something better, more loving, more lucrative, or more rewarding than what you're afraid of losing.

When you can understand this distinction and release the pattern of seeing yourself as finite and separate, you can move into your essence, experiencing your true brilliance. You'll make very different decisions because you're no longer confused about your true state.

ACTIVATING DEATH

Releasing the fear of loss can give you the opportunity to have more neutrality. It allows you to both choose and to also accept what it is.

What do you need to release?

14. TEMPERANCE

ELEMENT: Fire

Present moment, patience, resiliency, integration, equanimity

The Temperance card is a welcome sight after the intense transition and clearing of the Death card. Temperance seeks to baptize you, cleansing you of the past and rebooting your life. Temperance asks you to take stock of what is still standing and to assess if it is aligned with your highest purpose.

The two cups held by the angel are the key symbol on the Temperance card, similar to the infinity symbol seen in The Magician and Strength cards. The central figure is an archangel, although there is some disagreement in the tarot community about which archangel. With a cup in each hand, the angle tempers wine (fire) with water.

Because the angel is balanced elementally and in present time, nothing spills. If there is a tight grip on the future or the past, the liquid spills. This symbolizes how any sort of attachment can create a big wet mess and block the flow of life.

This card can show up when you need to trust and be patient with a process, allowing it to unfold in its own time and in its own way.

In metallurgy, tempering is a process used to make metal such as a sword stronger by subjecting it to the greatest heat it can tolerate without reaching its melting point, then folding it, pounding it out, rapidly cooling it and then repeating the entire process. Again. And again. This process of extreme exposure tempers the metal, rendering it more flexible, less brittle, and therefore stronger.

Maybe you've just gotten your butt kicked by a major loss and you're barely sure which way is up. Maybe you just got thrown off the Wheel of Fortune ride or maybe you had some karmic debt to pay with Justice.

When you get this card, you can feel as if you've been in and out of the fire, tested, pounded out and just when you think you can't take anymore, you find yourself back in the fire for another tempering.

The person who draws this card upright can feel vulnerable and raw, like a newborn baby in some area of their life, and it is important to be gentle and patient with their process of becoming centered again in who they truly are.

The Temperance card is a card of hope and renewal. You didn't need all those artificial trappings of success, anyway. Now that you've been tempered, it's time to reassess probably darn near everything, but it's okay because there's nothing else more important to do.

Reversed Temperance

Imbalance, lack of moderation, extremist, polarity, intolerance

When the Temperance card is reversed, it simply means imbalance. Look to the surrounding cards for a better understanding about how the imbalance is manifesting. The imbalance could refer to a lack of moderation, substance abuse or self-abuse, such as eating too many cookies, wallowing in unhelpful emotions or picking the same fight. It can also mean controlling or being controlled.

Maybe you continue to make the same mistakes over and over. Perhaps you're lacking in self-awareness or are trying to find a shortcut instead of allowing for the tempering process.

You may feel disconnected spiritually or not present in your body. Maybe an earlier process was not completed, such as fully grieving the loss represented in the Death card.

One frustrated woman repeatedly drew this card. She was in a tempestuous relationship, deeply in love one day and then unable to tolerate him the next day. The minute he did, or didn't do, something she didn't like, she threatened to end the relationship.

She was driving herself crazy by telling herself she should break up with him for a litany of reasons, but then running to him for comfort and support, getting close, and then repeating the pattern.

I suggested she stay in her "intimacy workshop" and commit to not breaking up or mentally entertaining breaking up no matter what for three months and then see what happened. When you can break a major pattern, there are usually some good nuggets of gold underneath.

When she didn't let herself break up or spin out mentally about how "bad" and "wrong" he was for her and instead chose to be in the relationship, the whole relationship shifted.

She had major realizations about how she avoided intimacy and practiced being more authentic in his presence. The relationship eventually ended, but it fell off naturally without drama as a byproduct of her being in the present moment, like the angel in the card.

The Temperance card reversed means there is a sense of impatience with the process. You may feel as if you're paddling upstream and fighting the flow of life. It can help to stop trying to control an outcome or imposing your ideas about what is right. Instead, surrender from strength.

ACTIVATING TEMPERANCE

Your body is the best ally to stay in the present moment because your body is right here, right now in the space and time continuum.

Try noticing an inanimate object and then where a specific part of your body is in relation to it. Or see if you can feel the space between your toes.

What are you noticing right here, right now?

15-21 EXISTENTIAL LESSONS

THE LESSONS of the last seven cards in the major arcana are existential. They teach you about sovereignty. Not the sovereignty represented by the Empress or the Emperor, but the true sovereignty represented by the World card, where you float in the center of life, free of illusions and fully present in the space-time continuum.

The Devil is happy to point out any area where you forgot your connection to pure source. Once you have that awareness, there's no going back, and the Tower levels any outworn notions of false identity in order to create a sound foundation.

After the destruction of the Tower card, comes the reprieve of the Star card, granting a glimpse of the limitless possibilities and the ultimate reset.

The Moon and Sun cards help you align with your highest purpose which leads to the transcendent awakening represented by the Judgment card, allowing the Fool to complete the journey in the winner's circle of the World card.

15. DEVIL

Fear, addiction, habit, attachment, unconsciousness

After leaving the peace and clarity of the Temperance card, much like leaving the Garden of Eden, we meet our old friend, the Devil. This card may look scary, but the Devil can be quite helpful. What is scary is when we aren't aware of the Devil.

When the Devil card shows up, it represents an imbalance in the body and the spirit. The two figures are an inverted version of the Lovers card. They don't hold hands and they now have horns, showing they have lost the innocence depicted in the Lovers card.

The posture of the Devil is reminiscent of the Magician with one hand up and one hand down. But while the Magician taps into pure source, the Devil brings down damnation.

The placement of the two humans is also similar to the Hierophant, but they will not benefit from any supplication to the Devil. This is worshiping at the altar of all the wrong stuff - sex, money, power. Plus the seven deadly sins - pride, envy, gluttony, greed, lust, sloth, and wrath.

These may seem like really intense categories and you're probably thinking, I'm not that bad. And of course you're not "bad" at all. However, do you ever feel you have to sacrifice yourself for others? Should be more holy, right? Nope, that's the Devil. Fighting for the wrong cause? Not speaking your truth? Zoning out on games? There's the Devil again.

I mention these minor offenses because the Devil can be a visually intense card and difficult to explain to those who suffer so much from trying to be "good". Anytime you try to please, seek approval, are compliant or obedient, you're slow dancing with the Devil. You're compromising your truth and your sovereignty.

The Devil card can represent a person. If it does, this person may be slick or seductive. They may be a fast talker, telling you everything you want to hear. They may have missed receiving the conscience chip at the human factory. And they are likely taking advantage of you.

The Devil gets a bad rap, but the purpose of the Devil is to show us the ways we block consciousness through our bad habits, attachment to our stories, and our perceptions of reality. In the Ex Animo deck, the Devil is represented as a shadow puppet, created by our own hands, signifying that we are the creators of our own demons.

We've all consorted with the Devil. Maybe it manifested as an addiction to substances, people, or beliefs. Maybe you traded in hard work for the easy way out or chose gossip instead of communicating with integrity.

The Devil can represent anything you use to keep yourself numbed out or distracted, such as looking at your phone. Little by little, as we surrender our control and responsibility, we lose our connection with the present moment.

The Devil card can show addiction or self-deception issues. While most of us are familiar with addictions to sex, drugs, alcohol, or work, an addiction can be anything blocking your connection with pure source.

Addiction often has an existential crisis at its root. When you address the existential issue, often the habitual way of numbing the pain can change through connecting with pure source instead of trying to fill the void with a substance or behavior.

Even activities which seem innocuous, such as watching television, having a crush, or a supposedly fortifying activity such as reading, can be a source of addiction if we do them habitually, blocking you from having more experience. It doesn't matter what the activity is, but why and how it is being done.

Underneath these behaviors, there is fear and confusion about the nature of source and our connection with it. The person drawing the Devil card may feel unworthy or guilty. There may be confusion or limiting beliefs based on religion, lineage, or culture.

REVERSED DEVIL

Releasing limitations, changing negative patterns, getting rid of bad habits, letting go of fear

When the Devil card is reversed, it can mean you're breaking free of your limitations. Fear is no longer in the driver's seat of your life.

You may feel you have your life back and you get to decide what is best for you. You're making different choices and forging fresh territory in your life and relationships.

Maybe you finally stopped vaping and now you're dealing with all the feelings the habit was covering up. Maybe you set a boundary with your work hours. Or maybe you stopped answering the phone at two AM when your needy, crazy-making friend was calling to throw up all her problems on you.

If the Devil is showing up reversed, you're likely changing old habits and limiting beliefs. You have gained fresh awareness through removing the filters that were blocking your experience.

ACTIVATING THE DEVIL

Once the government catches a skilled hacker, they wisely add them to
their payroll. You can do the same with the Devil. Hire the Devil to help
you tighten up your commitment to your light. Just don't give the Devil
the keys to the control room.

What habits are blocking you from becoming more conscious?

16. TOWER

ELEMENT: Fire

Upheaval, breakthrough, breakdown, destruction, change, transformation

The Tower card means change. Real change. The blow-up-your-life kind of change. The kind you don't really want, like ever. Many tarot readers immediately thought of this card when the Twin Towers fell in New York on 9/11.

The Tower card depicts the biblical story in Genesis of the Tower of Babel which was built by Nimrod to avoid another flood and to reach Heaven in order to have ultimate power and buddy up with God. In the story, God smote the Tower of Babel because Heaven cannot be contained within the limitations of the material world. The Tower of Babel was symbolic of human greed, arrogance, and sin.

The Tower card is typically ascribed to Mars as the god of war and aggression, but can also be ascribed to Pluto, the planet of the underworld, and to Uranus, the planet of revolution.

No one welcomes this card. In theory, we want change and transformation, but it can be hard, messy, and uncomfortable.

When you're experiencing the medicine of this card, you can feel as if you're falling, your world is collapsing, and everything and everyone you thought you knew has to be questioned and reassessed. It can feel like the rug has been pulled out from underneath you. And it can be lonely, bewildering, and disorienting.

The Tower card can show you how your foundations and structures have been built on falsehoods and cannot support true growth. The Tower card is like remodeling a house and discovering there are termites and the whole structure will need to be gutted, while you're living in it.

Because most of your life is designed to avoid the root causes of suffering at all costs, it's difficult to allow your life to fall apart. But once you're leveled, it can be a powerful place for transformation.

By the time your life falls apart, you've been stripped of everything on which you normally hang your self-definition and self-worth represented by the Wheel of Fortune and Death cards. All of your normal "fixes" and distractions represented by the Devil card are gone. Your suffering comes down to a purely existential issue:

What is the point of my life?

This is the ultimate question we are all asking all the time. The problem is, it's usually covered up by the noise of daily life and we only have to face it in times of major crisis and loss.

The good news is once you face your deepest fears, then you can live your life more purposefully and more authentically. You get to live your life with less time and energy wasted on avoidance, overcompensation, distraction, and things that don't align with who you truly are.

REVERSED TOWER

Resistance to change, avoidance, suffering, delaying the inevitable, trying to hold It together

The Tower card can be even more difficult when reversed. It's knowing you need to throw up, but using sheer will to keep it down. It can mean resisting, avoiding, or fighting necessary changes.

Maybe you know you'd be better off if you ended your marriage, but you're staying put because you don't want to lose the illusion of the social or financial security you believe your marriage gives you.

It could be time to move, but you don't want to. Or maybe your budget was cut at work and there's no future for you there, but you can't quite bring yourself to resign just yet.

With the Tower reversed, there is pressure to change, and it's easier to heed it.

ACTIVATING THE TOWER

It's best to begin with the premise that your experience, whatever it is, is somehow perfect for you. So when you're forced to be in your dark place, this is a good thing because there is no escape. You're forced to be present with yourself and with your experience.

But how to be present with your experience? Here are a few tips.

1. **Try to be still**. Moving, whether physical or mental, can distract you from your experience.
2. **Breathe**. Simple and foolproof. You can even count your breaths if you're in a really tough spot. Or you can inhale to a count of four and exhale for six.
3. **Use your body to stay present**. Feel your feet, feel your spine, feel the inside of your left elbow, notice the details of your physical experience in the moment.
4. **Spatially Reference** by noticing where you are in relation to furniture, walls, sound or light.
5. **Experience your emotions** without a cast of characters and major storyline. Take a breath when you touch on a feeling and this will help you clear the emotion without becoming stuck in it.
6. **You can't do it wrong**.

What change have you been dreading that would make you feel more alive and authentic?

17. STAR

ELEMENT: Air

**Incarnation, field of all possibilities, purpose, unlimited
potential, hope, creativity**

After Death, the Devil and the Tower thoroughly kick your ass,
stripping you of your ego and attachments and identity, you're ready to
do the genuine work you were born to do.

When the Star card shows up, you're resonating with something much
bigger than you and you'd best pay attention. Most interactions with
stars feel significant and fated such as seeing a falling star. Your breath
catches and you quickly try to think of a wish commensurate with such
a rare astral event.

Star brings you in touch with your inner light and divinity. It shows you
how to create in the void where all unmanifested energy is and can come
into form. Star tells us we can harness the potential of the void and
create infinitely.

The Star card is beyond the Magician's rudimentary ways. It represents
your soul code and what you came here to do. It represents your
purpose, your blueprint, your soul connection.

Your genuine life can't begin until after who you thought you were has been destroyed and everything that isn't who you are, all of your excuses, habits, and limitations are gone. What is left is the Star.

When you draw the Star card, it's time to be the Star of your life. No more avoidance. All that devilish stuff got blown away with the Tower.

The lesson here is to be in full alignment with life, beyond who you think you are. This isn't a card of doing, but a card of becoming. Time is now an irrelevant, outworn, third-dimensional idea of the Hierophant you're way beyond.

The Star card can represent a trip or a restorative period when you get back in touch with yourself. When you simply explore and experience with no sense of urgency, no to-do list.

The Star can represent a conception or channeling, such as when a song or poem comes through you. Like the water being poured from the pool of the collective unconscious, you're simply providing the temporary container for the collective unconscious to make itself conscious.

Yes, you get to be the star with your message, but it's not your message. You get to light the way for others like the Star of Bethlehem. But it's not about you. If you still think it's about you, then you'll have this card reversed, or have to go back to the Magician and try again.

REVERSED STAR

Disconnected, hopelessness, misguided, uninspired, disillusioned, disengaged

When ships used to navigate by the stars, it would be difficult when clouds covered the sky. It can feel as if you've lost your bearings when the Star card is reversed. Or you think you're following a star, but it turns out to be a satellite.

We all have a built-in compass helping us navigate life, but the directions can become lost in all the noise of daily life and the opinions of others. The Star card reversed could tell you to stop caring about trying to do it right.

Star reversed could mean you need to dream bigger. Or stop deferring or downgrading your dreams. When you realize you're divine, you have no excuse for not loving and approving of every freckle of yourself completely.

It could mean that you are not heeding the promptings of the universe. Or that you think you know better.

The Star card reversed could tell you it's time to be the star in your own life instead of letting others upstage you. It can also mean you're too busy mucking around in day-to-day life to look up at the stars and ponder the infinite possibilities available to you.

ACTIVATING THE STAR

It's time to shine your unique light. The world has been waiting for you. When you make the choice again and again to focus on your own brilliance, despite the chaos, negativity, spinning, and turmoil that tries to pull you down, you train yourself to live your life more and more from your natural brilliance.

What is your dearest wish?

18. MOON

ELEMENT: Water

Unconscious, dreams, illusion, past life, psychic development

A bright, full moon dominates this card. The Hebrew letter, yod, rains down, signifying divine gifts and power. There are two pillars with water and the moon between them. The same pillars are in the background of the Death card, but the pillars are larger and closer in the Moon card, with moving water between them.

The water in the foreground represents the collective unconscious and universal pool of truth also seen in the High Priestess, Temperance, and Star cards.

The dog symbolizes our social conditioning and civilized nature, while the wolf symbolizes our instinctual nature. Both are howling at the moon. The shellfish lives in both water and on land and carries the wisdom of the subconscious.

There is a yellow path between the dog and the wolf. As you follow the yellow brick road of your knowing and intuition, you walk the fine line between conscious and unconscious, known and unknown, tamed and untamed. Eventually, you find your way back home.

The moon gives off no light of its own, but it can reflect, bend, transform, and reshape light. The light of the moon is borrowed light, just like the reality the Moon card represents is a borrowed reality. In the Moon's light, friends may not look so friendly and enemies may be your path to enlightenment.

The moon dies and is reborn every 29.5 days. When you draw the Moon card, you're dealing with reflections, shadows, and projections. Astrologically, the moon represents the mother and the "womb door" we've chosen for this lifetime. In a reading, it can indicate that larger forces, such as karma, past lives, or ancestral patterns are at play.

If the Moon card is in a reading with a King, Queen, Knight or Page, it can mean there is a past life at play with the person represented by the court card with whom you still have some unresolved karma.

But you don't have to look beyond your current life to get the healing. Anyone with whom you don't have loving neutrality is in your life to help you heal something and to show you where you forgot your truth, your path, and your highest purpose.

The Moon can represent tapping into the unconscious through intuitive development, clairvoyance, or seeing auras. It may help you tune into your inner voice, dredge up repressed memories, or help you break through subconscious blocks. It may illuminate some unpleasant truths, casting them in its gentle glow so you can examine them.

REVERSED MOON

Confusion, delusion, deception, ignoring intuition, disconnection from reality

Things may not be as they seem when the Moon card is reversed.

Someone may deceive you or mess with your perception of reality. You may be in La La Land or under someone's spell.

Maybe you're ignoring your inner promptings and the messages you're getting. Maybe you're unconsciously perpetuating and repeating the ancestral patterns or karma.

Maybe you're too open to other realms and have a hard time staying in your body. Maybe you've got psychic hitchhikers. Or maybe you're too empathic and have become a psychic dumpster for people. If this sounds familiar, then the practice of consciously occupying your body or strengthening your auric shield can help.

The Moon card reversed could mean you're stuck in a swampy quagmire of emotions. Or have an aversion to looking at your shadow and doing the messy work of healing. Moon reversed can show unproductive altered states of reality, such as the ayahuasca journey you wish you hadn't taken.

Maybe you have a low tolerance for woo woo or no interest in spirituality and instead prefer the "solid", black and white, spreadsheet reality of the material world.

The Moon card, both upright and reversed, can represent issues with the mother, or motherhood. It can mean issues with the menstrual cycle in women.

For many people, there is a natural awakening of innate psychic abilities. The age differs for everyone, but it is usually around 40 to 50. Often, the awareness follows a painful life lesson or two. The maturity gained from the suffering provides a stable container to handle the heightened awareness.

There also needs to be solid integrity before psychic information will be accessible. As long as you're seeking to know psychic information for the wrong reasons, the information will be blocked. It's like an integrity firewall. When your ego is involved, then the firewall will block you from tapping into the information available to all of us all the time.

True psychic abilities are developed as a natural byproduct of awakening. They can be developed without going through hell and back, but they will not be holistically integrated if the initiate has not done their healing work.

ACTIVATING THE MOON

Dreams can be a powerful tool for awakening, as "reality" is just another dream state and can be used to transform your waking life. Keeping a dream journal can help you tap into your subconscious.

Simply keep the journal by your bed and write whatever you remember from your dreams as soon as you wake up. Over time, you'll remember more of your dreams and you'll notice patterns and themes that you can use to navigate your awake world.

What are your dreams trying to tell you?

19. SUN

ELEMENT: Fire

Radiance, success, joy, vitality, triumph

The Sun is large, radiating its warmth and magnanimity upon all it touches. Sunflowers bloom, symbolizing the balanced ego. A naked child sits delightedly atop a white horse, symbolizing innocence and purity.

The child wears a crown of flowers, a red feather and holds a red flag, symbolizing victory and achievement. There is a gray wall and steps behind the figure showing hard work and the human structures that supported the endeavor.

The red flag is reminiscent of the mantle of the Magician and represents the manifestation of dreams. While the Moon represents the inner work you had to do in order to know and accept yourself completely, the Sun represents the expression of your authentic self out in the world.

The Sun is the nineteenth major arcana card. 19 contains the beginning represented by the number 1 and the end, represented by the number 9. The Sun card represents the confident, radiant sense of your individual Self, while remaining connected to a larger transpersonal Self.

Many interpretations of this card focus on papers and writing because paperwork used to signify the culmination of success, such as a contract, or a real estate purchase. One client drew this card along with the Fool card upright when asking about a job for which she'd recently interviewed. They offered her a job the next day.

REVERSED SUN

Read the fine print, ego-driven outcome, disempowerment, controlled outcome

A helpful way to remember the meaning of the Sun card when reversed is to imagine the clouds of your unresolved wounds blocking out the radiant expression of your natural brilliance.

When the Sun card is reversed, it signifies that the ego is out of balance, which can cause pride, egocentrism, insecurity, or wasting your potential on unworthy causes.

The Sun card reversed is exemplified by the myth of Icarus, who became overconfident and flew too close to the sun, melting his wax wings and falling to his death.

The Sun reversed reminds you to find the balance between ego-driven bravado and self-effacing, timid withdrawal. Both extremes lack a solid connection with your true self.

On the pragmatic side, when The Sun card is reversed, you'd better double-check the paperwork and be sure to read the fine print as the contract may not be in your best interests.

This card came up reversed a lot in my practice during the 2020 pandemic, as clients were seeking online courses of study and having a hard time distinguishing who was legitimate. Most times, the website and marketing looked promising, but there was no legitimate substance and it was not a wise investment.

A client drew this card reversed when she was negotiating a work contract. I suggested she review the contract again and sure enough, there were some major oversights for which she would have paid dearly.

Activating the Sun

Traditional goal setting doesn't always work in the ways you'd like. Sometimes it can feel like another way to beat yourself up. When you instead focus on clearing away the clouds of old stories that block your natural light, many of your goals will naturally be accomplished.

How can you radiate more of your true self?

20. JUDGMENT

ELEMENT: Fire

Ascension, awakening, realization, reckoning, atonement

The Judgment card denotes a reckoning of past choices and deeds in order to understand how they may or may not have served your highest good. Are you fulfilling the mission you signed up for when you incarnated?

The Judgment card heralds a new level of spiritual awakening where you realize a larger purpose for yourself and for your suffering. It's about being fully, authentically, and unapologetically you. No masks. No façade. Just you.

The Judgment card comes after the ultimate expression of the Sun card. The card shows men, women, and children rising naked out of their coffins with arms reaching up in exaltation, roused by the call of the angel's trumpet.

The figures rising from their graves no longer bear any trappings of the material world and are returning to the state of pure spirit.

The Judgment card depicts the Christian concept of Judgment Day, where it is believed that you will be judged for your choices and actions by a higher power.

For the person drawing this card, it can signify an opportunity to awaken from a limited consciousness and to rise from the ways in which you've kept yourself small or played it safe.

Maybe you spoke out about an unfair situation at work. Or maybe you took a major risk that breaks all the rules of your family system.

Whatever form it may take, Judgment tells you that your life is presenting you with an opportunity to awaken.

REVERSED JUDGMENT

False awakening, spiritual materialism, self-doubt, inner critic

The reversed Judgment card can simply mean poor judgment. Maybe you're deciding in haste. Or not operating in integrity. It could reflect poor judgment that you're regretting and beating yourself up for. There may be secrecy, guilt, or shame.

Sometimes when this card is reversed, it can represent a lack of discernment, such as not seeing situations or people clearly.

One woman who drew the Judgment card reversed was in a toxic relationship but felt sorry for them and explained away all of their controlling behaviors as coming from their wounds. While it was kind that she understood their suffering, it didn't excuse their behavior, and it didn't protect her from being hurt.

When the Judgment card is reversed, it can mean a false awakening. Or an avoidance of facing the truth. This is like the folks that talk a good, "love and light" game, but are miserable in their lives. They wield their spiritual resume like a sword and barricade themselves against authentic experience in their towers of spiritual elitism.

Chogyam Trungpa Rinpoche coined the term spiritual materialism to describe the appropriation or misapplication of spiritual practices to gratify the ego's desires. It can take many forms, such as self-improvement addiction, spiritual narcissism, pop spirituality, or cultural appropriation.

Another form can be spiritual elitism, using titles and experiences as resume builders in order to feel special or better than others. All of which spreads spiritual frosting over garbage without doing the true, deep, and often messy work of spiritual growth.

ACTIVATING JUDGMENT

If you listen to near-death experience accounts, there are some common components. One of those components is a life review. During the review, they all report seeing their life through the lens of love - how they gave it, missed it, lost it, or found it. After the review, they are left with the realization that love was always there and that it drove Everything.

The first step in forgiveness is recognizing that you were hurt. Next, you accept that you are hurt, and then you can feel better.

When true forgiveness happens, you rarely realize it because the past is no longer affecting you. It's as if you change the channel and tune into a higher frequency. The Judgment card is a call to let go of the past by changing the channel.

Like the life review, where everything is viewed through a lens of love, sins or mistakes don't matter in the same way. Of course, you can't bypass making things right if you have messes to clean up, but you don't have to whip yourself or others for eternity.

Are there any painful experiences you could view through a lens of love?

21. The World

Element: Earth

Wholeness, integration, ultimate success, fulfillment, accomplishment

The World is the last major arcana card. The Fool has made it through all of life's lessons and has come to the end of the journey, achieving the ultimate purpose of existence.

A naked figure in the center of a laurel wreath holds two wands. The laurel wreath symbolizes success and achievements. The red ribbons used to tie the laurel wreath form the sign of infinity, denoting an everlasting victory.

A flowing sash is wrapped loosely around the character. Like the Wheel of Fortune card, the four fixed signs of the zodiac, Aquarius, Taurus, Leo and Scorpio, are pictured in each corner. Unlike the Wheel of Fortune card, the World card has a fully realized being in the center. This being makes their own fortune.

The realized being on this card could not care less that others see them naked. They are comfortable in their skin and not worried about cellulite or age spots. Instead of being stuck on the wild ride of the

Wheel of Fortune, the being floats serenely in the center, the embodiment of success. They have power over the world, but the world no longer has power over them.

Pillars, reminiscent of the High Priestess, the Hierophant and Justice cards, are now double pointed wands held loosely in the figure's hands. The human definitions of success and the constraints of time and space have been transcended.

If you drew this card, you could feel as if you're on the top of the world. Fame and fortune may show up in some form with this card. Your achievements may make you a role model for others.

The World card could signify a literal or metaphorical graduation, or the completion of a project. It can mean traveling and seeing the world.

The World card signifies an expansion of consciousness. It's a well-earned, joyful card of having successfully navigated all the trials and tribulations of your path. It portends honor and celebration of your achievements.

REVERSED WORLD

Need for closure, limited viewpoint, world upside down, disappointment

When reversed, the World card can mean that your world feels upside down. Maybe you feel stuck and like nothing is going your way. Or you feel like Atlas, with the weight of the world on your shoulders. Maybe you finally achieved your goal but now you feel meh, like a deflated balloon.

Or, perhaps you're barricaded in your own little world, refusing to engage or adapt. The World card reversed can show an unwillingness to take a global view.

One client got this card after being wrongfully fired from his job. His identity and sense of worth was tied to his work, and he was lost without it. By taking a global view, he could still fight for his rights but also see that he was more than his job. He ended up making a major career change and was much happier.

The World card can mean delays or avoidance of completion. It can mean a lack of closure or that an unrealized dream or ambition may have had a faulty premise to begin with.

ACTIVATING THE WORLD

As the last card of the major arcana, the World card represents completion. Anything that is incomplete in your life can block you from being fully present. Incompletions can function like bookmarks, keeping you stuck in the past. Completion frees you to move forward in your life.

Is there anything in your life that is incomplete?

PART FOUR

THE MINOR ARCANA

There are 56 minor arcana, with numbered cards from ace through ten, and court cards, that include Page, Knight, Queen and King in each suit. The court cards are often re-named in modern decks, but the energy and lessons remain the same.

When interpreting the cards, the minor arcana will tell the story of how the major life lessons represented by the major arcana are playing out in your life.

There are four suits, each represented by an element and with common themes that connect them. Pentacles are connected with the element of earth and represent physical concerns. The swords represent air and topics related to thinking, communication and change. Water elemental topics such as love and emotion are represented by the suit of cups. The wands represent the element of fire and its energy, power and dynamism.

Each suit tells a story and when you first begin, I recommend laying out the cards of each suit in order from Ace to King and observe the progression of the suit as it begins with the ace, develops, and then completes the cycle. Bearing this in mind will enrich your experience of tarot.

Many approaches study the minors by suit, but I prefer to group them by Ace, Two, Three, etc. This grouping is in order to illustrate three things. One, to understand the universal cycle of each suit within its element. Two, how numerology plays a role in interpretation. And last, to help understand the different suits through contrast with each other at the same point in the universal cycle.

ACE

ACES REPRESENT BEGINNINGS.

In Numerology, the number One is the seed of opportunity in our lives. It's a groundbreaking symbol of confidence, power, and action.

Whether it is a new job or investment symbolized by the Ace of Pentacles, the brilliant new idea represented by the Ace of Swords, the Ace of Cups opening to receive more love, or the divine inspiration of the Ace of Wands, the Aces are the beginning of a cycle. Even if you feel afraid, the Ace inspires you to embrace new beginnings.

ACE OF PENTACLES

Element: Earth

Opportunity, health, investment, new job, new house, starting a project

A cloud with a hand offering a single pentacle hovers over a blooming garden. White lilies, representing innocence, idealism and purity of spirit, bloom in the foreground.

A yellow path leads out of the garden toward a blue mountain beyond, symbolizing potential and great rewards if the safety of the garden is left and the path is followed.

Pentacles are associated with the element of earth and represent earthly endeavors and experiences. The Ace of Pentacles is a seed that could grow if you cultivate it. In order to do so, you'll need to take the risk and go beyond your comfort zone.

Maybe the Ace of Pentacles represents the big account you just landed. Or you could be investing in real estate or starting a new business. The Ace of Pentacles signifies the beginning of something that could pay off later.

The Ace of Pentacles presents you with an opportunity on the earthly plane. The opportunity could be anything that correlates with earth, such as money, parenthood, property, health, or career.

Reversed Ace of Pentacles

Poor investment, waste of time, false promise, risk avoidance, missed opportunity

When the Ace of Pentacles is reversed, you may want to reconsider your investment of money, time, or energy. If the Ace of Pentacles is like a seed, then when it's reversed, it could mean that either the seed of your endeavor is a dud or that your soil is depleted. You may need to replenish yourself or take a break and lie fallow for a bit to charge yourself up.

Maybe the seed you have in mind is actually a weed or a seed that won't grow well in your current climate. Maybe the house you want to buy is a money pit or your new business idea won't be successful.

It could mean you're spending your money in ways that aren't supportive of your future, such as buying the latest phone when you can't make rent.

The Ace of Pentacles reversed could mean that you aren't paying enough attention to your physical body or that you're at odds with your physical body. Maybe you are having a hard time getting pregnant, or you struggle with your physical appearance.

Perhaps you aren't sleeping well, or nourishing yourself appropriately. Maybe you're being too hard on your body by exercising obsessively. Or maybe you're avoiding being in your body altogether. When the Ace of Pentacles is reversed, something in the physical world isn't functioning optimally.

Activating the Ace of Pentacles

In the poem, "Birches," Robert Frost writes, "Earth's the right place for love: I don't know where it's likely to go better."

The Ace of Pentacles is a portal to the materialization of goals, dreams, desires, ambitions.

What seed would you like to plant?

ACE OF SWORDS

Element: Air

New idea, fresh perspective, Aha! moment, clarity, truth

A glowing hand emerging from a cloud holds the Ace of Swords. The sword is upright with two edges that can cut both ways, showing an ability to see both sides of a situation.

There is a gray background with mountains in the distance symbolizing wisdom and ambition. Six yods surround the sword. Yod is the little shape that looks like an apostrophe, It represents the Hebrew letter for Y. Yod is the building block of all the Hebrew letters. Yods represent sparks or ignitions of divinity that form a creative beginning.

The tip of the sword is crowned, demonstrating divine thought piercing through the crown chakra, cutting clearly through any illusions in order to get to the truth.

Laurel leaves hang from the crown, representing potential for success and victory if the idea is carried through. The Ace of Swords starts the process that propels you to act.

The Ace of Swords represents a burgeoning new awareness. Maybe you have a brilliant idea for an app. Or you're finally setting a boundary with your work.

In its purest form, the Ace of Swords represents a download from the universe, especially if major arcana are also present, such as the Magician, the High Priestess, the Star, the Moon, Judgment, or the World.

You'll recognize the divine ideas represented by the Ace of Swords when you experience them because it can hit you like a lightning bolt out of nowhere while you're showering or driving, for example.

Or the idea may come to you in a dream. Some people may hear a voice clearly tell them the idea. In whatever way it shows up, it would be wise to pay attention and take action.

Reversed Ace of Swords

Bad idea, self-abuse, self-criticism, negativity, lack of strategy, poor communication

The Ace of Swords reversed can represent an idea that is hurtful or self-sabotaging. Most of the sword cards, when reversed, point toward the person looking at the cards. This is a key to interpreting the sword cards because a sharp weapon should be aimed away from the person using it in order to not cause self-harm. When it is pointing toward you, there's usually some self-inflicted suffering.

The sword cards can signify mental health issues such as worry, judging, or more extreme examples of anxiety and depression. The Ace of Swords reversed can mean self-abuse through self-criticism, negativity, or feelings of unworthiness.

For example, I read for a young woman who got the Ace of Swords reversed. She was pale and thin, almost skeletal. When I saw the Ace of Swords reversed, I talked about a new idea but that the idea was hurtful to her. She confided she planned to start a new restrictive eating regime that was clearly more of an eating disorder than a program for health and nourishment.

If the new eating program would have been healthy for her, then it would have likely presented as the Ace of Pentacles upright.

Activating the Ace of Swords

The Ace of Swords can help you gain access to other realms of awareness. Most truly innovative ideas are downloaded from here. These realms are always available to us through dreams, meditation, and other practices.

What is the universe whispering to you?

ACE OF CUPS

Element: Water

Opportunity for love, creativity, opening of the heart, connection, romance

Water overflows the Ace of Cups and streams into the world. Water symbolizes the astral world, where spirit and experience meet. The five streams represent the five senses.

The Hebrew symbol of the yod drips 26 divine drops. Yods represent the 26 letters in the alphabet, the building blocks of creation and communication. The white dove above the cup represents peace. There are lotuses beneath the cup symbolizing the purity of growth out of the mud of existence.

There are many theories about the letter "W". It is the 23rd letter of the alphabet and it most likely refers to the 23rd Psalm, "Thou preparest a table before me in the presence of mine enemies: thou anointest my head with oil; my cup runneth over."

If you are familiar with Christianity, then this image may remind you of the sacrament of communion, which is about connecting to the sacred within ourselves and the sacred within others. It also echoes the symbolism of the Holy Grail.

All the Cups cards are correlated with the element of water and the Ace of Cups is the quintessential essence of water. The element of water is associated with love, flow, emotion, intuition, and passion.

This is a full cup, so full that it runneth over and never runneth out. It's divine love, a love that is plugged into a limitless source. We all have access to the bottomless cup of love all the time. Unlike the human sources of conditional love, tapping into the pure love source brings you true fulfillment.

The Ace of Cups means that life is offering you divine love. It could be in the form of a puppy, a creative project, or it could be the beginning of a romantic relationship. It could also mean a reboot in an existing relationship where you've remembered the love and re-chosen to be together. Whatever it is, the Ace of Cups means you're letting more love into your life.

Reversed Ace of Cups

Neediness, emptiness, stuck, emotionally blocked, fear, loss of love

When the Ace of Cups is reversed, it means your cup is spilling and you're losing your precious essence. It can symbolize emptiness, frozenness, or flooding.

Maybe you're involved with an energetic vampire who sucks the life out of you. Or maybe you've been hurt and block yourself from receiving love and support. Maybe you cannot access your emotions or your emotions overwhelm you.

You could be enabling someone, keeping them weak and dependent on you so they don't leave you. Or you could be the needy one. The Ace of Cups reversed could signify a dynamic of dependency or insecurity. You may sacrifice yourself and feel unappreciated. Maybe you're trying to fill the emptiness of your cup with dark chocolate or hard seltzer.

Activating The Ace of Cups

If you want to experience more love in your life, a good place to start is your heart center. This is the area of your chest near your nipple line in the front and back and correlates with our ability to give and receive love.

Try paying attention to this area of your body throughout the day, especially around others. Notice what or who throws you out of connection with your heart and use your body to help you stay attuned with your heart.

How can you experience more love in your life?

ACE OF WANDS

Element: Fire

Passion, inspiration, initiative, energy, potential

A hand holds a wand, with ten leaves growing on it. The ten leaves are a nod to the Kabbalistic Tree of Life and eight leaves fall off the wand shaped like the Hebrew letter yod, symbolizing divine sparks.

There is a river with fertile land and mountains and a castle in the distance. The mountains symbolize ambition and wisdom. The castle in the background shows the potential for future success and accomplishment.

The Wand cards are associated with the element of fire and its energy, power, and dynamism. The Ace shows the initiation of potential beginning to be actualized.

The Ace of Wands upright is an all-systems-go, ready-to-launch card. It symbolizes all the qualities associated with fire - passion, creativity, drive, will, determination, and energy.

And yes, the wand is phallic. It can represent libido, passion, or sexual attraction.

Reversed Ace of Wands

Unmotivated, unfocused, misdirected energy, lots of sparks but no fire

The Ace of Wands reversed can represent a bad idea, like a firework that is a dud. It can symbolize a lack of energy or blocked energy.

While the Ace of Wands upright can feel like an espresso, the Ace of Wands reversed can feel as if you're drinking two pots of coffee all day, every day, frying your nervous system and you still can't muster up the energy to work toward your dreams let alone fold the laundry that's been sitting on the sofa for a week.

When reversed, the Ace of Wands can show that there may be competition, struggle, controlling, or forcing, rather than operating from divine inspiration as the source of motivation.

Depending on the surrounding cards, the Ace of Wands reversed can literally mean erectile dysfunction (the Knight of Wands reversed can also have this meaning). And even if it doesn't represent this exact physical manifestation, it is helpful to think of the card figuratively this way - you have desire and you want to do something with your desire; you want to consummate something, but you can't keep your momentum going long enough to get it done, or you lose your "life energy" prematurely. Either way, you're not able to perform how you would like.

The Ace of Wands reversed can represent nervous, unfocused energy or making a poor investment of your time. It could be an idea with no divine sparks. It could mean that your libido is on the fritz and needs to be sorted out.

As with all the wands, when reversed, there can be misdirected fire in the form of frustration, resentment and anger. Anger can be productive when appropriately directed, but when the Ace of Wands is reversed, it becomes either self-directed and internalized, such as beating yourself up, or else can come out sideways toward others in unexpected or unintentional ways.

Activating the Ace of Wands

The Ace of Wands can help you fire something up, whether it's a creative idea or an athletic competition. Place it on your desk to light a fire under your endeavors.

What lights your fire?

Two

THE NUMBER Two introduces the idea of duality. Each of the number Two tarot cards brings in a new dynamic to be integrated and balanced.

Unlike the number One, which is the number of beginnings and self, the number Two resonates with building, partnership, and coexistence.

Whether it is the balancing act in the Two of Pentacles, weighing two options in the Two of Swords, the introduction of another person in the Two of Cups, or the potential of the Two of Wands, each card seeks to harmonize and build upon the energy introduced by the Aces.

TWO OF PENTACLES

Element: Earth

Balance, weighing the options, indecision, commitment, responsibility

The character in this card wins the biggest hat in the deck award. Hats symbolize ideas, easily accessible intuition, and extensive knowledge.

The Two of Pentacles card feels similar to the Temperance card, where the angel pours the two chalices without spilling. In both cards, as long as you're in the present moment, all is well, despite the sometimes rocky seas of life depicted in the background of the Two of Pentacles.

The infinity symbol around the discs represents the material world with infinite possibilities and also the ebb and flow of material gain. The Magician and Strength cards also have the infinity symbol.

The Two of Pentacles may mean you have a choice to make and are weighing your options. It may be time for you to step back to have a better perspective of the situation in order to choose more wisely.

The Two of Pentacles represents balancing resources. Maybe you're trying to decide whether to volunteer for a cause that is dear to your heart, but doing so will take time away from your job and family. Or maybe you're trying to decide whether to rent or to buy a home. One client pulled this card when he had two job offers he was considering.

This card also reminds you that there is enough. Enough time, money, energy or whatever you need in order to proceed. All you need to do is to choose.

Reversed Two of Pentacles

Ungrounded, insecure, uncertain, distracted, imbalance

When the Two of Pentacles is reversed, the balancing act is over. It can mean that either a decision was made or else the precarious balance has been lost.

If a decision was made, look to the surrounding cards to understand the nature of the decision and whether it was supportive.

Weighing your options is a wise and healthy part of most decision-making processes, but when the Two of Pentacles is reversed, it can feel like spinning your wheels. The spinning is often because of a disconnection with one's center, which creates confusion and an inability to listen to your inner compass for guidance, resulting in an inability to choose.

Maybe you're overextended and overwhelmed. Maybe you're having difficulty prioritizing. Or maybe you have poor time and resource management. Perhaps you struggle with balancing your needs with the needs of others.

Sometimes people become stuck in perpetual fence-sitting and indecision, not realizing this is still a form of decision-making, albeit a disempowering one. It can mean being stuck in a loop and unable to move to the next level at work or with a project.

Activating the Two of Pentacles

The lesson of the Two of Pentacles is to help you take the next step in a process. Some part of you already knows the best answer and the Two of Pentacles can help you choose. Tapping into this card may present you with an option that hadn't existed before.

How can you trust your inner compass?

TWO OF SWORDS

Element: Air

Choosing, stalemate, confusion, inaction, a need for courage

The person depicted in this card needs to make a choice, yet they are blindfolded. How can they see clearly to make that choice?

The figure has water behind them, representing intuition and emotion. It's currently calm, but the jagged rocks show there is difficulty and the stakes of the choice are high.

The moon is also present, reminiscent of the High Priestess card, symbolizing access to wisdom, but also the potential for confusion.

The character's body posture gives a sense of being closed off, blocked or disconnected from emotions or from day-to-day life. There could be hiding of intentions, protecting of the heart, or maybe their emotions are blocking them from seeing the situation rationally.

They don't realize the power of the weapons they hold or are unwilling to apply them to their situation in order to gain clarity.

The Two of Swords shows there is a decision to be made, except you feel you can't decide or don't want to see the answer. The mind is divided and confused, pulled in two different directions.

However, like the character in this card, you have all the information and tools you need to make a decision.

The Two of Swords is associated with the sign of Libra, a sign known for seeking balance at all costs. Those who have a strong Libra influence in their astrological natal chart can be conflict-averse and have a tendency to disregard their truth in order to keep the peace, often being too nice or too accommodating.

The person who draws this card may be in an unhealthy situation or feel victimized and opt to sacrifice themselves in order to maintain whatever they consider "safe".

The temporary balance achieved in the Two of Swords may be accomplished by avoidance. Courage is required here and deeper work may be needed to achieve true peace.

Reversed Two of Swords

Clarity, decisive action, avoidance, helplessness, justification

The Two of Swords card is the picture of worry and anxiety. If you've drawn this card, fear may prevent you from taking decisive action.

When the Two of Swords is reversed, it can show that either a choice has been made, or it can be an intensification of the upright version, indicating hesitation to face a hard choice.

The Two of Swords reversed can be like your friend who complains endlessly about their job but doesn't take steps to find a new job. It can represent a pattern of self-abuse or blaming.

If the Two of Swords represents avoidance, then there can be a general sense of not taking responsibility for your life. Like the Two of Pentacles reversed, there may be indecision as a form of decision. There may be peacemaking, victimhood, compromising of self, or struggle with the balance of mind and the emotions.

If a choice has been made, it may feel like someone has harshly ripped the blindfold off and now you can see the truth. It can be hard, but luckily, you're holding two powerful weapons you can use to create the change you need.

Activating the Two of Swords

Confusion is a high state of being. It means that a new idea is challenging your old way of thinking. If you're trying to decide and feel stuck, try sitting in the posture depicted in the card, imagining a sword in each hand with your arms crossed, forming an X on your chest. The letter X represents your inner authority. Then imagine taking off the blindfold, standing up, and facing your problem with both swords drawn and ready for action.

What choice would you make if you knew you couldn't make a mistake?

TWO OF CUPS

Element: Water

Connection, Romance, Friendship, Communion, Kindred Spirit

The Two of Cups is one of the main relationship cards in tarot. It illustrates two people connecting, each holding a cup near their heart that they offer to the other. Hermes' caduceus hovers above the couple in the sky, symbolizing alchemy and that divine chemistry is present. The chimera above the caduceus further underscores a larger purpose to the union.

Meetings represented by the Two of Cups can feel destined and the person you meet can feel like a "soul mate" or uncannily familiar. Often there will be a court card near the Two of Cups showing who the love connection is.

One client drew this card along with the King of Pentacles a week before she ran into a middle school classmate she'd had a crush on 20 years previously. She was thrilled to discover he'd held a secret flame for her too. As they became reacquainted, they resonated with each other deeply and truly.

She reported back that she was shocked by how easy and natural it felt to be with him despite so much time passing. Her previous long-term relationship felt more like a brother and sometimes a child, but this felt deep and real. It wasn't all roses, of course, but the heart and soul connection remained strong and true.

The connection represented by the Two of Cups card does not have to be romantic. It can represent your best friend, a like-minded colleague, a supportive neighbor, a classmate or any heart-based connection with a purpose to the union that is bigger than both parties individually.

With the Two of Cups, there is an air of respectful teamwork, with both parties interested in mutually benefiting from the outcome. Both people are better because of being together.

Ideally, relationships represented by this card are born out of mutual respect and admiration, and are filled with understanding and love.

Reversed Two of Cups

Broken relationships, breakups, blocked connection, losing that loving feeling

When the Two of Cups is reversed, the love spills out. This could look like broken promises, a breakup, lack of trust, or general disconnection. Maybe there is an inability to be vulnerable, an imbalance of power, or codependency.

It can mean looking for love in all the wrong places or being stuck in a loop with someone who isn't good for you.

Maybe you're giving and giving but not receiving anything in return. Or maybe you've abandoned your dreams in order to stay with someone. Healthy love shouldn't require sacrifice or control.

The Two of Cups reversed can be painful, and it may be helpful to think of your suffering like an intimacy workshop with the other person teaching you how to be present with your experience.

Drawing the Two of Cups reversed doesn't necessarily signify a break up. It can mean that you've had an argument or that you're working through some issues. Maybe you are blocking love and need to re-choose and re-meet each other from a new place.

When the Two of Cups reversed is accompanied by the Lovers reversed, it's more likely to be either a total reset or a true parting. Here, even though it can be hard, it is usually for the best.

Activating the Two of Cups

Healthy relationships are rarely portrayed in popular culture. Most popular songs, for example, are based on codependency, victimhood, sacrifice, or control.

In your beloved's presence, you may feel more alive or excited, but that is you allowing you to experience more of yourself in their presence, and not because of the other person.

How can you become your own soulmate?

TWO OF WANDS

Element: Fire

Possibility, adventure, enterprise, travel, goals, what's next?

Based on the clothing and stance of the character depicted in the Two of Wands card, they have achieved a certain level of success and are now gazing outward from a position of security to see what is next. The character holds the entire world in their hands.

The wands on either side represent creativity and responsibility which form a gateway to the world. The flowers in the turret symbolize innocence and idealism (white lily) and passion (red rose), the union of desire which becomes manifestation. White and red flowers are reminiscent of both the Magician and the Hierophant cards.

The character stands on top of a human-made structure, meaning that society, convention and institutions have granted this vista. The rooftop location also shows that they've reached the top and are ready for the next step.

If you've drawn this card, you may need a challenge or quest. Somewhere to direct your energy. The Two of Wands tells you to go for it, whatever it is. But wait, what exactly is it you want to go for? Oh yeah, right, that's the problem.

This card comes up a lot when there are questions about next steps in a career, business, or education. I read for a high school student who was trying to choose a college to attend. She was torn between a university that was close to home so that she could take care of her father and brother or going somewhere further away that was a better fit for her and what she wanted to study.

She drew the Two of Wands upright when she looked at the school farther away that she truly wanted to attend. We shuffled thoroughly and then looked at the option of staying close to home. This time she drew the Two of Wands reversed. It still surprises me how the same card out of 78 cards can show up even after shuffling or when using a different deck.

When the Two of Wands is upright, you hold a world of potential in your hands, all you have to do is choose.

Maybe you're considering a career change or a move to London. Or maybe you want to hike the Appalachian Trail. The Two of Wands asks you to choose the next direction your life will take. It requires careful consideration of which choice is most in alignment with the original, divine inspiration represented by the Ace of Wands.

Reversed Two of Wands

Stuck, avoidance, unactualized potential, lack of clarity, risk averse

When reversed, the Two of Wands can show avoidance of taking the next step. Fear of change or fear of loss may be at the root of the avoidance.

Maybe you're clinging to comfort instead of taking a chance. Maybe you don't feel ready or are wasting your time and energy in a dead-end job instead of pursuing your ambitions.

The Wands are associated with fire, and when fire isn't consciously directed, it can die out or explode. Active avoidance can manifest in many forms, such as anger, anxiety or depression.

The person who draws this card may feel overwhelmed or afraid of making a mistake and instead misses opportunities.

The Two of Wands reversed is the symbolic (or literal) equivalent of being stuck living in your parents' basement. It's time to launch out of the nest, and see what you can do out in the big wide world.

Activating the Two of Wands

The shift from potential to actual can be daunting, but it's more painful if the energy stays stuck instead of being realized.

If you don't know or if you feel stuck, just take a step, any step, no matter how small. Your path is always where your feet are. This will move energy which can help you gain clarity. Then, train yourself to enjoy feeling more alive.

What step can I take right now toward my dreams?

THREE

THE NUMBER Three symbolizes the principle of growth. When the initiating force of the number One unites with the germinating energy of the number Two, there is fruitfulness.

The Threes in the minor arcana show pivotal moments where energy is being released to either expand or to dissipate. Each of the Three cards takes the sources of energy in the Aces and the Twos and adds a foundational factor that involves others.

The Three cards are dynamic, and show that change is afoot. Threes deal with creativity and growth. Like all tarot cards, this can go in different directions. Take the celebratory Three of Cups, for example, compared with the dire Three of Swords. Both cards deal with the expansion of the heart and with love, but in very different ways.

THREE OF PENTACLES

Element: Earth

Plays well with others, good work well done, conscious collaboration, co-creation

The Three of Pentacles depicts collaboration and hard work. The character in this card proudly displays their work to others who look on with interest and approval.

The Three of Pentacles represents the physical act of creation, of making something out of nothing. The Three of Pentacles grounds creativity in the act of doing, anchored by hard work, often in relation to others.

The person who gets this card is good at the work that they do. Whether their work is paid or unpaid, they are a contribution to the world, with their efforts being acknowledged.

Maybe you're bringing innovation to your work. Or you're working with a group to research and write a paper. Whatever you're doing, you're doing it well and your good work is being noticed by others. You may not be compensated fairly just yet, but your work has some alignment with your purpose.

The Three of Pentacles represents a successful beginning toward achieving your goals. It can also remind you of the value of collaboration. When you integrate diverse viewpoints, experiences and expertise, you can achieve more.

Reversed Three of Pentacles

Disengaged, unappreciated, left out, meaningless work, unworthiness

When the Three of Pentacles is drawn reversed, it can signify a lack of confidence in work, feeling unappreciated, or having difficulties working with others.

Maybe you're being excluded from a project, or you're feeling stuck with uninspiring work. Maybe you're not able to do the work you know that you're capable of because of limiting social dynamics, such as favoritism. Or maybe the group with which you're trying to collaborate isn't a good fit or simply isn't productive.

When the Three of Pentacles is reversed, it could signal that your primary motivation is seeking approval or negative attention from others in order to define yourself and your value in the world. If you give someone the power to approve or disapprove of you, then you've placed yourself in a vulnerable position. It rarely feels good and it certainly won't lead to success.

The more confident and worthy you intrinsically feel, the more you'll easily be able to share your gifts with the world and to consciously collaborate and co-create with others.

One client drew this card when he was frustrated with his job. He had inherited complicated and annoying accounts, requiring the most hand-holding, so his volumes weren't as high as his co-workers despite his higher quality and quantity of work.

Because he was so competent and knowledgeable, his co-workers came to him for help instead of their manager. The manager assessing his performance was threatened by his competency and regularly went to social events with his coworkers, but didn't include him.

When we dug deeper, he realized that he'd never gotten any appreciation for supporting his mother and sisters when his father left them. He connected the pattern with his intimate relationships, where he would rescue women but was left feeling used. In order for him to be able to successfully collaborate with others, he was going to have to give up his need to be heroic and start from scratch.

Within a month of his reading, his boss moved away, he was promoted, and he met someone who was not in need of rescuing.

Activating the Three of Pentacles

When limiting beliefs are running your life, it can be challenging to collaborate with others because you don't feel worthy or like you have the right to express yourself.

How can your expression be a gift?

THREE OF SWORDS

Element: Air

Suffering, grieving, loss, compassion, heart opening, heart healing

The scene in the Three of Swords card is bleak. The sky is gray and rain is pelting down. Not a pleasant scene, but often confirming the misery the person who draws this card is experiencing. The Three of Swords shows pain and suffering and there's no way around it.

The Swords symbolize thoughts and their ability to cause pain to your heart. Separation and loss can come in many forms, physical death being the most severe, but it could also be the loss of a relationship, an identity, a belief, a community, a dream, work, health or loss of purpose.

The loss doesn't have to be big, dramatic or negative. The Three of Swords can show up when a parent goes back to work after the birth of a child, for example, or following a positive move to a dream location. Even loss and sadness in the distant past can still be pertinent and inform the present.

Unfortunately, the dominant culture of the United States doesn't acknowledge and support the grieving process and how necessary it is in order to be fully human.

Buddhists dedicate meditation and study to death and loss in order to become more awakened. A Buddhist teacher with whom I studied spent many nights in graveyards in order to face the fear of loss.

Ideally, people are changed by suffering and loss, rendering them more open, compassionate, empathetic, aware, and alive. It can be bloody and painful and ugly, but it can transform you if you let it.

The beauty of this card is that it rips your heart wide open and, in the restoration process, your capacity for love becomes greater.

Reversed Three of Swords

Incomplete grieving, fear of loss, holding on, pushing love away, hardened heart

When reversed, the Three of Swords can signify an incomplete, stuck, or avoided grieving process. It could represent a closed heart. The surrounding cards will offer clues about the nature and cause of the pain.

Maybe you've been hurt in relationships and have shut down in order to protect yourself. Or maybe a relationship is over, but you don't want to let go and move on.

One client drew this card when wondering when she'd finally have another intimate relationship. She drew the Three of Swords reversed because she was still stuck in an incomplete grieving from her divorce ten years previously. When I suggested that there might still be something stuck from her marriage, she was sure that she was fully over it.

I asked her if she'd be willing to delve a little deeper to see what the Three of Swords was about since it was blocking her from having the new relationship she wanted. Sure enough, her ex-husband came up as the King of Cups reversed. Some developmentally stuck areas from her childhood also showed up which had contributed to the demise of the relationship.

She hadn't been aware of her contribution to the problems in the marriage, and gaining clarity allowed her to complete her grieving process and move on with her life. She met someone soon after.

Activating the Three of Swords

Few of us take the time and space to grieve completely. If you're blocked in any area in your life, it may be because of an incomplete grieving process.

If this card has shown up for you, consider any major losses that you've experienced and check in with yourself and see if there is anything that needs to be healed or completed in order to move on.

Do you have any tears left?

THREE OF CUPS

Element: Water

Party time, celebration, community, connection, your tribe

Under a clear blue sky with bounty at their feet, the three characters in this card joyously dance. Their cups are full, and they are celebrating.

The suit of Cups symbolizes love, emotions and heart-based connections. The Three of Cups represents feeling positively connected with others in your tribe. This card looks like a good time and it is a good time. It often signifies a party.

Maybe you're going to a wedding or a family reunion. Or it could be as simple as coffee with a like-minded coworker. One client drew this card representing a visit to the community barn where they kept their horse.

There are many social engagements that won't trigger this card in a reading because it only shows up when you're going to have a communion of souls where your heart is touched by others.

Reversed Three of Cups

Miscommunication, feeling left out, disconnected, isolation, a dreaded social obligation

The Three of Cups reversed can be the opposite of fun. It's like that party where you feel awkward, wondering how much longer you need to stay in order to be polite.

The Three of Cups Reversed can represent a party that is being dreaded because of the people who will be there, or a party that falls short of expectations.

Maybe it's a party gone wrong such as overindulgence or overspending. Or maybe you feel left out. It can mean the cancellation of a party, a party missed, or going to an event out of a sense of obligation or duty with no expectation of a good time.

A client pulled this card reversed in the future placement representing a graduation party she was dreading because her ex-husband and his family were also going to be there. Since she was obligated to go, I asked her if there was a way that she could turn the card around. Could she still have a good time despite her former in-laws?

The question led to a deeper realization about how much she reacted to outside circumstances and allowed them to dictate her experience. She went to the party and reported back that it was fine, but that fine was an immense improvement.

Activating the Three of Cups

If you're looking for your tribe, struggling to build community, or to have healthy friendships, you can meditate on this card to release fears about connecting with others.

Who are the kindred spirits in your life?

THREE OF WANDS

Element: Fire

Game on, possibility, what's next, action springing from an idea & commitment

If you compare the Two of Wands with the Three of Wands, you'll notice that both cards show a successful figure with their back to you surveying a scene.

In the Two of Wands, the figure is on a rooftop, considering what is possible and choosing a course of action. In the Three of Wands, the figure has committed to a plan with their feet firmly planted on the ground.

The character has developed beyond the rumination and germination stage represented by the roof of the castle and is now bringing the idea out into the world.

In this card, you can see the process of moving into a phase of action. It's as if the character has moved out of their parent's basement and is ready to build their own life and home.

The Three of Wands is about taking action. It heralds a time of expansion, growth, commitment, and taking the next step toward the realization of your dreams. You've got the vision, you've done your preliminary work or study, now you're putting it into action to make it happen.

One client got this card when he published the website for his business. Another client got this card as they were planning to build a house. It can represent any endeavor as it becomes actualized.

Reversed Three of Wands

Avoidance, unfocused, frustration, immaturity, fear of commitment

When the fire of Wands doesn't get expressed, it can wreak havoc internally as self-criticism or as self-sabotaging behaviors. It can also be unfocused energy, ricocheting in the mind with no traction or grounding in real life.

When the Three of Wands is reversed, it can show an unstable, unsustainable foundation for an endeavor. Fear may underlie delays in your project. Or maybe you're playing it safe and not taking enough risk.

When parents ask about a child and this card shows up, it can mean the child is struggling to be successful in a traditional parenting or education model. The child may be a kinesthetic learner, for example. Or simply a healthy child who would rather move their body, or be outside, or learn by doing, instead of sitting still and staring at a screen.

It may seem like these kids have issues with authority or can't focus, but the real problem is that the system is broken. The system is too limited and doesn't support the child to develop in the way they are hard-wired to develop. The stronger the will and spirit of the child, the more the system demands compliance. Many of these kids are star seeds, coming in to forge new paths for human evolution, but it can be a frustrating loop for them.

When the Three of Wands is reversed, there is likely a need for discipline, not in a punishing way, but in a helping-you-to-focus way.

Activating the Three of Wands

If you want to be successful, you'll have to exercise some discipline and control. Maybe it's time to pay your dues or maybe you just need to put in the hours to develop your ambition.

If you're feeling stuck in your life, you can start with your breath and develop discipline through awareness and control of your breath, which will then inform the rest of your life.

What area of your life could use more focus?

Four

THE NUMBER Four symbolizes the principle of putting ideas into form and structure. The goal of the Four is to stabilize and establish order, which allows ideas and plans to manifest into material form.

In the Four of Pentacles, the character is grasping his earthly possessions while the character in the Four of Cups is containing themself. The Four of Swords depicts a character in a state of recovery, in contrast to the Four of Wands, which builds a structure to contain energy and ambition.

FOUR OF PENTACLES

Element: Earth

Overattachment, overidentification with physical material world, controlling, scarcity, greed

A figure with the hallmarks of traditionally defined success sits with their back to the city, clinging tightly to four pentacles. If they could talk, they would probably say, "Mine! Go away."

This character's pentacles have given them the illusion of security, and they have oriented their life and body around protecting and holding onto the pentacles, closing off and turning their back on their community.

The tight hold on their pentacles blocks them from experiencing life. The pentacle on their head shows that they have lost their connection with spirituality. A pentacle by their heart blocks authentic, heartfelt connection with others, creating a barrier to giving or receiving fully.

The two pentacles under their feet block the connection with the earth and with nature. They have numbed themselves to humanity in order to hold on to the illusion of security.

The Four of Pentacles can represent over-attachment to possessions, to physical appearance, to health, or even to "owning" another person.

In life, the Four of Pentacles can represent behaviors and habits that numb you from connection with life, such as compulsive shopping, fear of germs, or constantly checking your phone. It can represent pursuing a false definition of success.

When there are deep feelings of unworthiness, it is common for there to be an overcompensation to give the external appearance of success. For example, maybe you never felt good enough, so now you wear an expensive watch to prove to the world that you've made it.

The figure on the card has defined their life through their experience in the physical plane. They may have lost their connection with their authentic self in achieving external sources of validation.

When I studied in Tibet, I was with a woman who constantly took photos. As part of her healing, we suggested she try to spend a full day without her camera. When she did, she was surprised by how naked she felt. She realized how much she hid behind her camera and how much fear came up around missing life by not being able to "capture" memories.

The minute you seek to capture or remember something, you become attached and out of present time and space. The Four of Pentacles reminds you of a need for spiritual evolution. It's time to understand that there is more to life than money, status, a toned body, a fancy car, or a trophy type relationship.

Sometimes, the selfish posture of the Four of Pentacles can represent significant progress from being a doormat and getting used by everyone. Maybe you've sacrificed and given too much and now you can't receive, or vice versa. Either way, the flow of life is blocked.

There could be hoarding with this card, which is an unconscious behavior in response to deep feelings of insecurity. There can also be overspending, plastic surgery, keeping up with the Joneses, name-dropping, or any other behavior that leverages the material plane to offset deep feelings of insecurity and unworthiness.

On the other end of the spectrum, some people aren't attached enough to the physical plane and need to learn how to deal with basic human needs of food, clothing, and shelter. Sometimes this card can tell you to be more grounded and oriented toward the earthly plane, such as building a savings account for emergencies.

Reversed Four of Pentacles

Trusting life, receiving, letting go, generosity, engaging

When the Four of Pentacles is reversed, it can show that you're feeling like you're worthy and you believe you're enough. You no longer need externalized reference points to know that you're acceptable.

The reversed Four of Pentacles can show that you're more open to others and are sharing resources more freely. It can also mean you're opening your mind to the possibility of realms beyond the material plane. Maybe you've stopped your distracting behaviors and are available to connect authentically with others.

Or, like all the cards when reversed, instead of being the opposite of its upright meaning, it can represent an intensified version of the upright meaning. If this is the case, it could show a deep insecurity, scarcity mentality, obsession, compulsion, or that you're really dug in and stuck in the materialistic realm.

Activating the Four of Pentacles

If this card is talking to you, remind yourself that you're intrinsically secure, there is enough, and that you're enough. It could be helpful to do a deep dive on your belief systems around money.

If you make decisions based on fear and lack, try thinking of paying bills as a form of expressing your appreciation.

What would you do if you knew there was enough time or money?

FOUR OF SWORDS

Element: Air

Rest, illness, time out, shutdown, reset, recovery

This is one of the gloomier looking cards, with an image of a sarcophagus. People can get a little scared when they first draw it, but it simply means a need for temporary withdrawal from life.

The Four of Swords card has some similarities to the Hanged Man card. They both represent a forced time out for a good cause. The Hanged Man is for the higher purpose of integrating the life lessons meted out by Fortune and Justice, whereas the Four of Swords is because you've likely burnt yourself out and need some time to chill and integrate.

The Four of Swords follows the Three of Swords which represents suffering and loss. After a major loss, it can take time to heal. Often you feel overwhelmed and don't have the energy or desire to engage in regular life. You can feel beat up and bruised and just need some space and downtime to process.

Emotions that aren't processed consciously are stored in the body and then you can get stuck in a depressed state or else you process the emotions physically as an illness.

When I see this card in a reading, I ask if the person has been sick recently. They will often answer affirmatively. It can be just a little cold, or something more serious, but if you look closely at the cards, you may see what triggered the emotions that led to the sickness.

The "time out" can take many forms - illness, social withdrawal, depression, exhaustion, or hibernation. I've even seen it mean incarceration.

Both reversed and upright, this is one of the top mental health indicator cards, depending on the surrounding cards. Especially when the Four of Swords is reversed, it could represent depression or anxiety.

Reversed Four of Swords

Burnout, deficit of self-care, need to slow down, stress, overwhelm

When a period of rest goes on too long, the Four of Swords can mean stagnation. It can show the effects of stress, inadequate self-care, long-term illness, or self-harm.

When the Four of Swords is reversed, you're on the road to burnout, if you're not already there. If you don't take the time to rest and rejuvenate, then your life will force you to.

The Four of Swords reversed can mean you're disengaged from life. Maybe you're numbing yourself with an addiction. Or maybe you hide in your work. Maybe you're depressed.

Look at the surrounding cards for more information about the nature and cause of the timeout.

Activating the Four of Swords

When your computer or phone slows down or starts to glitch, the first step is to shut it off. The second step is to wait before turning it back on. This approach solves most problems.

The Four of Swords is telling you to shut down and give your body and mind a chance to reset itself.

How can you reset yourself?

FOUR OF CUPS

Element: Water

The teenager card, oversensitivity, emotional attachment, self-protection, overreaction

The character in this card appears to be privileged. They are well-dressed and appear contemplative under a tree and not toiling in a field like other kids their age. The character's body language is closed off, and they look sullen.

Meanwhile, the Universe is offering a miraculous gift they can't receive because they are wrapped up in angst and focused on everything that's Wrong.

The figure in the Four of Cups is unwilling to engage in life and do what it takes to be happy and fulfilled.

The Four of Cups is the Teenager Card, because some teenagers can seem critical, ungrateful, and self-absorbed, causing them to miss opportunities for growth, learning, adventure, and love. In the teenage phase, nothing is good enough and they don't want to work for it. Or talk about it. Now leave me alone!

The developmental task of the teenager is to leave the nest of their family and discover who they are in the world. They do this by testing their boundaries and engaging with the world in their search for truth. Many of us never complete the developmental task of leaving our family of origin's home and seeking our truth.

In the zodiac, each of the signs represents a stage of development, Aries, for example, being the baby and Capricorn being the elder. The sign of Cancer is considered the teenager of the zodiac and the Four of Cups is associated with the sign of Cancer.

The crab represents the sign of Cancer, and those with a lot of Cancer in their astrological natal chart can display a tendency to retreat into their shells which is what the Four of Cups is portraying. Often the person who draws this card is attached to emotional security and doesn't want to jeopardize the known by taking a risk. They would rather hide in their safe shell.

Maybe you're stuck in a negative rut and can only focus on what is wrong in your life. Or maybe you're too busy gazing at your navel to live your life. It's easy to become so overly focused on your internal process and feelings that it prevents you from authentically interacting and noticing the surrounding magic.

The Four of Cups can manifest as pettiness, stubbornness, and apathy. It can signify a poor attitude with defeatist thinking, such as believing that nothing ever goes your way.

The Four of Cups can show a tendency to be locked into one-dimensional thinking and being unable to see the possibilities in the present moment.

Like the Four of Pentacles, there can be feelings of lack and stuck energy. Like the Four of Swords, there can be unprocessed emotions. These tendencies can manifest as controlling behaviors to keep life at arm's length.

Reversed Four of Cups

Gratitude, willingness, openness, engagement, hope

When the Four of Cups is reversed, the character reaches for the proffered cup with a spirit of adventure and gratitude. The teenager has grown up and makes their bed and takes out the garbage without being asked because they want to.

Maybe you broached that uncomfortable conversation with the person you've been dating. Or maybe you took the risk and volunteered for a high-exposure project.

If you've drawn the reversed Four of Cups, you're taking responsibility for your life and for your choices. You're no longer wallowing in self-pity or protecting yourself by avoiding engagement with life. You're likely feeling a sense of hope and gratitude for the opportunities that you've been given.

Conversely, the Four of Cups reversed can also mean an intensification of the upright version, meaning disengagement and retreat even further into a protective bubble.

Activating the Four of Cups

Notice how often you use closed body postures such as crossed arms or legs. Are there specific situations where you're more closed off? If so, try uncrossing and opening your body and see how it changes your experience.

What opportunities could you open up to receive?

FOUR OF WANDS

Element: Fire

Stability, social structure, home improvement, reliable foundations, success

The Four of Wands is one of the cheerier cards in the deck. There is an image of a chuppah, which is a traditional part of a Jewish wedding, with a happy couple raising their bouquets. The card has a yellow background. It's sunny and everyone is happy.

Success, prosperity, stability, security and laying down roots are all themes of the Four of Wands. It can represent teamwork, community spirit, or families coming together.

The Four of Wands can represent weddings or events, especially if the event marks a building of security or a new partnership. It can also signify coming home and reunions. Any type of event where you fit in and feel welcome.

The original spark of the Ace of Wands is taking shape in the Four of Wands. Four is the number of stability and structure. This card can represent a literal house or a containing and defining structure, such as a marriage or business. This card can indicate home improvements.

Even minor home improvements such as rearranging furniture, transforming a guest room into an office, or painting a bathroom can register as the Four of Wands. Maybe you're moving in with your significant other or putting your house on the market. Maybe you're renting a new office space.

For children, I've seen this card represent their bedroom or their classroom at school. In one reading for a child, the Four of Wands represented a new seating arrangement. In another reading it showed the change from elementary school to intermediate school. Both of which were a big deal from the kid's perspective.

It doesn't have to be an actual home. It can mean an office or a business or a project that is finally getting some legs and taking off. For one client, the Four of Wands represented a social media venture, including a new podcast.

Reversed Four of Wands

Housing woes, renovations, instability, conflict, insecurity

When the scene of the Four of Wands is upside down, the four wands resemble a prison. A sense of imprisonment can be a helpful way to understand its meaning when reversed. The Four of Wands reversed means a lack of security and structure in any realm, but it often manifests in the dwelling or work space.

Maybe you're underwater with your mortgage or your house has been on the market for over a year with no offers. Or maybe you're overwhelmed by repairs. Maybe you can't find an affordable place to rent or you're stuck in a rental contract. Maybe it's not a physical house but your family structure, which is making you feel stressed or trapped.

The Four of Wands reversed can also mean delays and setbacks. It can indicate a scattered focus with too many irons in the fire. There may be procrastination or you could feel you're not getting any traction with a project. Maybe you completed a major undertaking, but you don't feel you're getting the recognition you deserve.

In a love relationship, the Four of Wands reversed could signify conflicting agendas. Maybe you're considering moving in together, but there are complications or delays. It could mean either you or your beloved is getting cold feet. Or there may be a fear of commitment.

Whatever it is, the dominant theme will be instability.

Activating the Four of Wands

The place where you live reflects your mind. Look around your home and see what you notice. Does it feel warm and inviting? Chaotic or cluttered?

Maybe it's time to get rid of those photos of your ex or toss the science experiment growing in your fridge. Holding on to possessions beyond their "expiration date" can keep you stuck in the past.

Is there anything that it's time to release?

FIVE

THE NUMBER FIVE SYMBOLIZES CHANGE. Five is the pivotal point between the numbers one through nine and represents a variety of experiences through its developed senses.

The Fives of tarot offer many opportunities for making positive life choices and learning life lessons through experience.

Each of the Five cards in tarot has to do with change, conflict, and challenge. All the cards bring the energy of their respective element to a head, whether it's the competition in the Wands, conflict in the Swords, the destitution of the Pentacles or the emotional desolation of the Cups. Each of the Fives represents a key turning point.

FIVE OF PENTACLES

Element: Earth

Struggle, impoverishment, outcast, excluded, not enough

Two destitute figures trudge through the snow. One figure is barefoot, and the other is wounded and uses crutches. It's snowing, and the background is black and cold. They wear ragged clothes. The only color comes from inside the church through the stained glass. There is a sense of being left outside of the warmth, support, nourishment, and community represented by the glow coming from inside the church.

After the miserly compensation for the inner experience of feeling impoverished depicted in the Four of Pentacles, comes the full-on experience of impoverishment. The characters in the Five of Pentacles are struggling to survive.

The Five of Pentacles represents insecurity in all of its iterations. Most frequently, the inner sense of impoverishment and lack felt by the person who draws this card leads to external struggles with lack, such as lack of time, love, support, health or money.

The Five of Pentacles card doesn't necessarily mean there is financial lack. People who draw this card can have a huge balance in their bank account and all the trappings of success and wealth, but the underlying fear is that there isn't enough and that they aren't enough.

Maybe you're feeling left out socially. Or maybe you lost your job and you've been hitting the pavement hard, but still haven't secured a new position. Physically, the Five of Pentacles can represent an injury or illness that sidelined the person from their life.

The key with this card is the light coming through the stained glass window. If these characters could understand that abundance comes from consciousness and true abundance can never be lost, they'd be completely transformed.

Reversed Five of Pentacles

Hope, a light at the end of the tunnel, recovery from loss, improvement, overcoming adversity

When the Five of Pentacles is reversed, the snow becomes the top of the card, appearing brightly like light and hope. The stained glass window, when reversed, appears to be transformed into an entry to recovery.

The Five of Pentacles reversed can be hopeful and can mean that things are looking up. It could mean the recovery from illness has begun or that finances are recovering, and that stability is on the path to being regained.

Many successful people have gone through bankruptcies, divorces, illnesses, failures, and other deep struggles. Most credit their success with their ability to adapt and grow from their challenges. In losing everything, they often discover what is truly worth living for.

Or you could be doubling down on your misery with sacrifice and struggle with a smattering of resistance to positivity and feelings of low self worth.

Activating the Five of Pentacles

When you see this card, you may want to remind yourself that abundance is a natural byproduct of your connection to pure source.

Your subconscious beliefs about money block your connection with true abundance and create your current relationship with money.

How am I already abundant?

FIVE OF SWORDS

Element: Air

Conflict, struggle, fighting back, deceit, self-serving, lack of conscience

In the Five of Swords, there has been a battle and a person gathers up the weapons with a smug expression as others walk away dejected. The skies are harsh, with jagged clouds, and the figures walking away in defeat are wearing yellow, symbolizing intellect and spirit.

The winner picking up the spoils of victory is wearing green and red, the colors of strength and passion, but also of greed and materialism.

The Five of Swords is the next step after the recuperation of the Four of Swords, where the figure was lying in a church recovering from the deep heart wounding of the Three of Swords. After recovering in the church, the character is ready to go back out into the world and may need to fight in order to regain territory or to change limiting belief systems.

The Five of Swords is about conflict; whether it is destructive or constructive depends on the surrounding cards and what you're going through. Perhaps you've been in a controlling, abusive relationship and after seeking therapy (the Four of Swords), now need to stand up and fight back to reclaim your self worth and sovereignty. Or maybe the battle is internal and you're struggling with self-destructive behaviors and need to banish the bad habits.

One unwanted side effect of the misapplication of spiritual principles is becoming enamored with your garbage, and wasting time and energy journaling about every banana peel and coffee ground. The Five of Swords can remind you to clean up the garbage. It may be time to roll up your sleeves and do whatever it takes to make things right.

You may have to get uncomfortable. Burning a name on a slip of paper will probably not get you the $15,000 back that they stole from you. Giving up your legal right to an inheritance in order to avoid conflict doesn't protect the relationship, it perpetuates the problems in the relationship.

You may need to make the call, file the claim, or report the perpetrator. Constructive conflict is healing and can be the most sacred, loving, and holy action available.

Or this card can mean you're involved in a pointless battle and you'd best cut your losses or shift the energy away from the source of conflict. Sometimes people argue because they need to be right. In these cases, not engaging in battle and instead choosing peace, love and understanding may be the path.

With the Five of Swords, someone may be manipulating a situation to their advantage. It's possible that you are the one rigging a situation or taking what isn't rightfully yours. You may be controlling or bullying in order to get your way, but you may not recognize your behaviors.

Or maybe the other party is controlling or bullying you to get more than their fair share of a deal. With the Five of Swords, the other party could take their ball and go home, leaving the collaborative table.

The Five of Swords can represent compromise, but not in a balanced way. The type of compromise signified by the Five of Swords represents a situation where one person got their way and everyone else gave up or gave in. This card comes up a lot in unpleasant legal negotiations.

The key with the Five of Swords card is to either show up fully and engage in constructive conflict, such as speaking your truth and standing up for yourself, or else to rise above the ego-based pettiness of the squabble and to look at the bigger picture of why this is happening and what is really at stake.

Reversed Five of Swords

Detente, avoidance of conflict, the silent treatment, losing what's rightfully yours, cold war

When the Five of Swords is reversed, it can mean you're working to repair damages with relationships. It can mean you're shifting a fighting dynamic into a constructive conflict.

Maybe you're successfully building your confidence and are pushing back. Or maybe you're dreading and delaying a necessary conflict that would ultimately be healing. You or the other party could be shut down and refusing to engage.

One client drew this card about a relationship. After a promising start, her beloved suddenly put on the brakes. He was not yet fully divorced and didn't want to jump into a committed relationship so quickly. She still had to see him every day and function publicly as co-workers. The Five of Swords reversed in her case represented the silent conflict and the hurt feelings still lingering.

Or, the Five of Swords reversed can mean an even more intense version of the upright Five of Swords, possibly with less self-awareness and even more destructiveness.

Activating the Five of Swords

Making things nice and keeping the peace is rarely authentic and can cause more damage. Many of us were conditioned to avoid conflict and anger. Yet anger can be your best ally in a healing process because it alerts you that your essence has been violated, and it motivates you to do something about it.

Are there any battles that you're avoiding?

FIVE OF CUPS

Element: Water

Disappointment, grieving, regret, self-pity, holding on

A character shrouded in black looks down at three cups which have spilled their green and red liquids. The sky is gray. Behind the figure, two upright cups remain. There is a flowing river with a house on the other side and a bridge in the distance.

The Five of Cups is about grieving and loss. The person who pulls this card is probably feeling sad and disappointed, possibly devastated. But all is not lost. There is hope because two cups remain standing.

In the Five of Cups card, the person has withdrawn from society and is now separated by a river from connecting with others. The bridge over the river symbolizes a new beginning once this character can shift awareness to what remains instead of focusing on what was lost.

Maybe you are still licking your wounds over the end of a relationship. You know it's ultimately best for you it's over, but it still feels bad that they cheated on you. Or maybe you were overlooked for a promotion you deserved and you're carrying a grudge, even though the person who got the promotion inherited a public relations nightmare.

It's possible to over identify with your losses, even using them to define yourself. When this happens, you may remain stuck in the past and never move on because you see your life through the lens of what has been lost.

Reversed Five of Cups

**Moving on, letting go, PTSD, victimhood, overidentification
with old stories**

Reversed, the Five of Cups suggests taking steps to shift the focus and
cross the bridge, moving on from devastation and loss. It can feel like
picking up the pieces with a heavy heart and starting again.

Or, it can mean not surrendering to the grieving process in order to
complete and move on. Both upright and reversed this card can
represent bitterness and resentment.

You could be stuck in an emotional loop or an old story, wallowing and
not making progress. It can also show overidentification with the victim
role.

Depending on the surrounding cards, there could be a doubling down
on the avoidance through putting spiritual frosting over the challenging
experience, instead of processing it consciously.

Activating the Five of Cups

If you find yourself making a cast of characters and petitioning your
internal panel of experts to agree that you have indeed been wronged,
then you may be exacerbating an already sad situation. Rubbing salt
into your own wounds isn't helpful.

Try to find your "bridge" by focusing on the two remaining cups. You
can do this by choosing to engage more with life and focus on what is
working.

*How can you unhook from the hurt and move toward hope and
faith in the future?*

FIVE OF WANDS

Element: Fire

Competition, challenge, ambition, conflicting agendas, struggle

The Five of Wands says, "What's next?" after the achievement and success in the Four of Wands. It may even say, "This is boring, let's blow up this popsicle stand."

As the harmonious structure of the Four of Wands wears off, the characters can feel restless. You can only laze by the pool for so long before feeling a need for change and challenge, especially with the element of fire.

Fire is expansive, and in the Five of Wands, fire can spread in an uncontrolled manner. In the Five of Wands card, the characters are fighting with each other and no one is winning.

The Five of Wands is the middle of the wands suit and represents a turning point in the evolution of the wands. The Five of Wands can mean that the person who drew the card, having experienced the comfort and stability of the Four of Wands, now wants to try themselves out in the world.

Maybe they run for political office. Or maybe they play lacrosse. Whatever the choice, they join the fray. Much like rams, they are compelled to figure out who they are by butting up against others in competition.

There can be frustration and anger associated with this card, but the struggle depicted in the Five of Wands is usually healthy and necessary for your evolution. Good competition makes you better.

The Five of Wands has a theme of comparison to others. This is a Leo card and the sign of Leo contains a fair amount of competition, pride, and ego. Am I the best? Are you the best? Who is the best?

With both upright and reversed, there can be issues with not fully expressing yourself, unworthiness, and not feeling good enough that need to be worked out.

The struggle can also be internal, such as procrastinating, lacking focus or spending time and energy on wasteful activities that don't help you progress toward your goals.

Reversed Five of Wands

Pointless struggle, jealousy, avoidance of conflict, red tape, spinning out

When fire isn't directed or focused, then there will be sparks flying everywhere, but no fire. The Five of Wands reversed can represent someone who is always busy and overwhelmed, maybe working three jobs but still can't make ends meet and continually postpones their dreams.

This can be the committee who can't decide because there are so many competing viewpoints and no one can listen or understand the other perspectives.

This can be the person who seems to have one problem after another, a crazy-maker who enjoys struggle, drama, and chaos because they lack inner authority and struggle helps them to avoid experiencing something deeper and more true.

This card can mean constantly getting sidetracked by petty disruptions. Or caught up in red tape and unable to make progress. It can feel like spinning your wheels getting nowhere.

The Five of Wands reversed can also have the opposite meaning of rising above the fray or a release from stress and struggle.

Activating the Five of Wands

Often the activity or experience we dread the most is the one that gives us the most personal growth.

When you challenge yourself, you expand the edge of your comfort zone and discover that you're more capable than you imagined.

When was the last time you challenged yourself?

Six

THE NUMBER Six represents community and connection. Love, harmony, healing, understanding, belonging, and caring are themes with the number six.

The big lesson with the number Six is relationships with others and learning how to give and receive support in a balanced and healthy way.

The Sixes in tarot are about recovery from the climactic devastation portrayed in the Fives. The Sixes provide solace and each card does it in its own unique elemental way.

The Six of Pentacles gives material support while the Six of Cups gives emotional and communal support. The Swords make mental movement away from struggle, and the Six of Wands finds a victory out of the fray depicted in the Five of Wands card.

SIX OF PENTACLES

Element: Earth

Giving & receiving, generosity, social responsibility, charity, caretaking

A wealthy figure hands money to beggars who kneel in supplication. They hold a balance in one hand and coins are being distributed with the other hand.

As an earth element, pentacles can represent earthly expressions such as money, food, land, or the physical body. The Six of Pentacles represents giving and receiving in society and the fair distribution of resources.

When you draw this card, it can mean that money is coming into your life, such as a bonus, a raise, a tax refund, an insurance payout, or a settlement. If it is upright, then the money received will be fair and will correct an imbalance.

If the Six of Pentacles doesn't represent money, it can represent some other form of support from society such as your neighbor picking your kid up from school, or a friend letting you sleep on their couch while you get back on your feet.

Reversed Six of Pentacles

Over-giving, imbalance of resources, inability to receive, unsupported

When reversed, the Six of Pentacles card can symbolize over sharing of your resources. Or giving in a way that isn't balanced and healthy for you. It may not be money. It could be your time, your attention, or your energy.

Maybe you're giving more than you're receiving. Check in and see if you're caretaking or enabling. The Six of Pentacles asks you to be fair to yourself and to others.

Another dynamic that's possible is defensively giving to avoid the discomfort of receiving, because accepting things from others makes you feel vulnerable.

Maybe you're volunteering too much. Or maybe you're giving too freely of your expertise and need to charge more. Maybe you feel you're sacrificing yourself, or that you're being taken advantage of.

The Six of Pentacles reversed can represent a lack of self-care or self-respect which leads to not getting the money, attention, and support you deserve.

Conversely, The Six of Pentacles reversed can signify that you're getting support, money or attention that you don't deserve or that you're getting it unfairly.

One client drew this card reversed when she knowingly "worked the system" to receive unemployment payments despite being capable of working.

Another client drew this card reversed after a messy inheritance, where he received more money than his sisters.

Activating the Six of Pentacles

An interesting experiment to see what is hiding beneath the habit of over-giving is to take a break from giving.

Try showing up at a party empty-handed, for example. If you receive a compliment, don't quickly say, "Thank you" and deflect with a compliment back. Instead, try taking a breath and allow yourself time to fully receive the kind words.

What are some areas in your life where you could receive more?

Six of Swords

Element: Air

Moving on, rite of passage, transition, personal or spiritual evolution, safe harbor

In the Six of Swords, it's time to pack up and get out of Dodge. After the battle in the Five of Swords, the characters have picked up their swords and moved on.

This is the archetype of an immigrant leaving their country in search of a better life. The journey abroad may be precarious, but necessary.

Moving away from everything you've known isn't easy. It takes courage and determination to head for unfamiliar shores. Often, the person who draws this card has been through an ordeal and the change they are making is hard won.

The two figures huddled in the boat are reminiscent of the two figures in the Five of Pentacles, who were also in desperate straits. It's key to note that there is calm water on one side of the boat and turbulent water on the other side, showing the potential for either a smooth or difficult transition.

The Six of Swords is about supportive change. It can represent a physical move, or it can represent a transition to a different state of mind. Whatever the move is, it will generate a different outcome in your life.

Often, a new mental framework will correlate with a new physical space externally, but not always. One client drew this card when they upgraded to a different role and desk location within the same company. Another client pulled this card when the company physically moved to a different floor of the same building.

The move doesn't have to be dramatic. It could represent a rite of passage. Or leaving behind a belief system, behavioral pattern, or relationship no longer serving you.

When the Six of Swords is upright, it means moving away from an unsupportive environment because you outgrew it. It signifies that your lessons were learned, and it's time to move on and start fresh.

Reversed Six of Swords

Forced change, resistance to change, running away, stuck, internal change

When the Six of Swords is reversed, the move, whether it's internal or external, can feel like it's through rough water. Maybe you're being forced to move under duress. Or maybe you're overreacting to an event, failing to be objective.

One client drew this card reversed when she was searching for housing after ending a long-term relationship. It hadn't sunk in that she could no longer afford her old lifestyle and she was looking at housing that would break her new budget. Once she accepted her new reality, she found the perfect and affordable place to start her new life.

There may be under-reacting and staying stuck when it's time to move on. Or maybe, instead of leaving the past behind, you're bringing your past with you.

When reversed, the rough water can represent hyper-emotionality such as running away, creating drama, or avoidance, rather than a strategic approach that supports your true evolution.

Activating the Six of Swords

Moving into unfamiliar territory can be disorienting, but it is an opportunity to let go of limiting beliefs, habitual reference points, and triggers.

Like clearing out a hard drive to help it work better, the key is to confirm the deletion of the old programs that no longer serve you.

What outworn aspects of yourself would you like to leave behind in order to move forward?

SIX OF CUPS

Element: Water

Warm fuzzy, nostalgia, hope, community, solace

This card is about feeling connected with others and the warm feelings that belonging can generate. In this sweet scene, two children share a cup with white flowers growing out of it, symbolizing innocence and spiritual connection.

The sky is clear and blue, and the scene is set near a well in a town center. A gray figure walks away in the distance, the specter of adulthood and a character you'll also see in the Seven and Eight of Cups.

After the devastation of the Five of Cups, now there is hope for the future. The Six of Cups is the scene that was in the distance of the Five of Cups card once they processed their loss and crossed the bridge toward the village.

If this were a card from a modern deck, it would probably have puppies and kittens in it and chocolate chip cookies, maybe comfy slippers and Sunday dinner. It represents a sense of healing, comfort, and belonging.

The Six of Cups can be like looking at the photo album or yearbook in order to remember that you're loved. It can be like finding solace in a supportive group. Or like your inner child got a bear hug.

Reversed Six of Cups

Forgiveness, letting go of the past, obligation, regret, accepting support

If you imagine the six cups upside down, they would be empty, so this could correlate with feelings of being emotionally fried and depleted. You might not be able to engage with others just yet. It could mean you're not seeing the support that is there for you.

The Six of Cups reversed could mean you're in a situation where you don't feel safe or supported. It can mean you simply feel left out. You may be experiencing loneliness or the postpartum period following a pregnancy. Perhaps you're emotionally drained following a major event.

The Six of Cups can show up reversed surrounding parenting issues or when a child switches households.

Maybe you've forgotten how to have fun. Or it could mean you feel homesick or broken and could use some tender loving care.

Activating the Six of Cups

Many obligations have a greater cost than benefit. When you feel obligated, it can feel as if you have to sacrifice yourself for the benefit of others. Obligations can be based on guilt and shame, and they can be self-destructive.

Sometimes obligations are simply what love requires, but if you find yourself consistently in situations where you feel imprisoned or weighed down by your obligations, it may be helpful to see what is underneath.

You might have a subconscious thought that if you make yourself indispensable, then you won't be abandoned, for example. Or that if you're really important and needed by others, then you're lovable.

It's not possible to help anyone by burdening yourself. Instead of getting into their sinking boat with them, be a lighthouse and become a beacon by which they can guide themselves to safety.

Are there any areas in your life where you are sacrificing yourself needlessly?

Six of Wands

Element: Fire

Victory, success, achievement, accomplishment, recognition

The Six of Wands is a triumphant card. A crowd cheers a victorious figure crowned with laurel leaves sitting atop a horse. A wreath hangs on their staff, heralding victory. This scene represents the type of success that is socially recognized.

The person who draws this card emerged successfully from the fray represented in the Five of Wands. They likely fought long and hard to earn their success and deserve the positive attention from their victory.

It can represent a graduation, an engagement, an award, or an achievement that is publicly acknowledged. Maybe you ran a marathon or finished your thesis.

One client drew this card after being given a promotion. Another client got this card when they made the varsity tennis team at their school. In an interesting case, a woman drew this card when inquiring about a major love interest. She was competing with another woman to "win" a man. The man-prize left his wife for her, so she "won", but she ultimately lost because he ended up doing the same thing with another woman a couple of years later.

Reversed Six of Wands

Arrogant, approval-seeking, vainglory, downplaying accomplishments

Wands symbolize the direction of fire, will, ambition. When reversed, it indicates that the will is being misdirected or not directed at all. There can be significant disappointment and frustration associated with this card.

The Six of Wands reversed could mean trying to achieve something for the wrong reasons such as seeking external sources of validation instead of feeling internally secure.

It could mean you feel shy about being seen and acknowledged publicly and as a result are hiding your brilliance. Maybe you are masking your accomplishments with false modesty. Conversely, it could represent undeserved recognition such as a stolen victory.

The Six of Wands reversed could highlight arrogance, overconfidence, or bragging. It can symbolize being a sore loser or a rude winner. It can signify loss or something that was attempted, but not achieved.

In the case of the woman competing with another woman for the man cited above, she drew the Six of Wands reversed at a reading a year later regarding the same relationship.

The Six of Wands may remind you that you haven't paid your dues and need to re-enter the fray portrayed in the Five of Wands and redirect your energy toward your goal.

Activating the Six of Wands

Some people are afraid of having their brilliance seen and will go to great lengths to hide. Others seek attention from anyone who will give it to them. When you're secure inside, you naturally want to share yourself with others in a balanced way.

How do you share yourself with the world right now?

SEVEN

SEVEN IS the number associated with wisdom and magic. It's the number of soul-searching, introspection, and analysis. The vibration of number 7 can feel secretive, private, and can be a loner. After the various forms of recovery portrayed in the Six cards, each of the Seven cards is getting ready for the final stretch in their own way.

The Pentacles are toiling and tending to their project patiently. The Seven of Swords is employing strategy, questionable though its resourcefulness may be. In the Seven of Cups, you can see a time of introspection leading, hopefully, to a choice. And with the Wands, there is a fight to stand your ground.

SEVEN OF PENTACLES

Element: Earth

Steadfastness, patience, gestation, investment, daily practice

A figure rests, gazing at the pentacles growing but not yet ripened. The character appears fatigued and patiently wonders when they'll get to harvest the fruits of their labor.

After the destitution of the Five of Pentacles and the beneficent recovery of the Six of Pentacles, the Seven of Pentacles works hard and invests wisely. The budding pentacles show that their hard work is paying off, but isn't ready to be harvested.

This card can feel like the messy middle of a project where the end is in sight, but you're still toiling away, feeling impatient to complete. It can also mean putting in the practice and paying your dues toward the mastery represented in the Eight of Pentacles.

The Seven of Pentacles is reminiscent of the fable of the tortoise and the hare, with the Seven of Pentacles representing the slow but steady effort that wins the race. Since Pentacles often represent money, this card could literally mean saving or investing money for the future.

The Seven of Pentacles could symbolize a physical goal, such as training for a race or showing up on your yoga mat every day for your spiritual practice. It could represent a pregnancy or the gestation of a creative project. The Seven of Pentacles is about taking the long view and putting in the work.

Reversed Seven of Pentacles

Short-sightedness, lack of commitment, lackadaisical, inattentive, overspending

When the Seven of Pentacles is reversed, it can show an unwillingness to put in the work that is necessary to get an intended result. There can be an element of entitlement or indolence when this card is reversed, where you're unwilling to do what it takes to achieve your goals.

The Seven of Pentacles often shows up reversed when someone just spent a large amount of money unexpectedly on a car repair, for example, and drained their savings.

Or it may reflect poor management of financial resources, where reserves are constantly being drained. One client drew this card after overspending on their wedding and then buying a house they couldn't afford. She and her husband had both grown up in a wealthy area with a lot of disposable income and failed to realize that they would need to build their own wealth.

The Seven of Pentacles can represent an accumulation of debt and a need to look at your spending habits or plan better for the future. There may be underlying feelings of financial insecurity.

The Seven of Pentacles reversed can signify the squandering of time on wasteful pursuits or endeavors that won't ever bear fruit. It could be a dead-end job where you're working hard but with no measurable results. One client drew this card when she was funding her boyfriend's get-rich-quick scheme that never panned out.

Activating the Seven of Pentacles

We often plant seeds without knowing what they will become. Will it be a carrot or will it become an oak? We have to allow our ideas to germinate and gestate in their own way, on their own timeline.

This doesn't mean abdicating responsibility or allowing your attention to waver. It's about giving loving attention to your life while knowing that it's in the process of becoming.

What is unfolding for you, and how can you trust your process?

SEVEN OF SWORDS

Element: Air

Strategy, deception, manipulation, scheming, coercion

The character in the Seven of Swords has stolen five swords and is tiptoeing away while looking over their shoulder. In the background are tents indicating that this character is operating outside of society for their best interests.

When this card shows up, you'll want to be wary of ulterior motives that may not have your best interests at heart. Things may not be as they seem. Do a thorough background check before hiring. Be sure to read the fine print before you sign any contracts.

The Seven of Swords can represent any sort of strategic or sneaky behavior, such as withholding, hiding, lying, avoiding, sweeping under the carpet, or simply not acknowledging the elephant in the room.

Maybe the person who draws the Seven of Swords is employing subterfuge, manipulating a situation to their benefit. Or maybe someone close to them is not being forthright or honest. It's common that the person drawing this card may not recognize and take responsibility for their lack of integrity.

The Seven of Swords is not necessarily dishonorable. The actions may be justifiable and a means to an end, such as secretly preparing for a divorce from an abusive spouse but being strategic in order to ensure your safety. Or maybe you're interviewing for a new job, but can't alert your employer because it would jeopardize your current job.

The Seven of Swords card can show a taking advantage of others, or profiting from others' loss. For example, a year before the US housing market crash in 2008, I read tarot cards at a holiday party for a sub-prime mortgage company and many of them drew the Seven of Swords because they were profiting from a broken system. Most of them didn't realize what they were taking part in.

The Seven of Swords can reflect feelings of guilt. It can mean overcompensating for not feeling good enough. Maybe you are pretending to be someone you're not, or lying and cheating on your commitments to yourself.

The Seven of Swords is a minor card and can mean something relatively innocuous, such as hiding your new shoes from your partner to avoid an argument. However, this card is a common ingredient when people are in denial, usually accompanied by the Devil card upright and some cup cards reversed.

Reversed Seven of Swords

Exposure, getting caught, self-deception, justification, gaslighting

Reversed, the Seven of Swords can mean that the deception was discovered and now the situation needs to be corrected in order to get back into integrity.

Or, it can mean that the deception is internal and you're deceiving yourself. Maybe you pride yourself on being open and honest, yet you aren't expressing your true feelings in a relationship because you're afraid of loss.

Or maybe you're controlling someone else's view of reality in order to "protect" them from the truth because you think it would hurt them or they couldn't handle it.

One client got this after she discovered that her elusive and always very busy with work boyfriend had another girlfriend. He vehemently denied that it was serious with the other woman, but based on her social media it was clear the other woman perceived him to be her boyfriend. Here, the Seven of Swords reversed represented him deluding himself and my client about the nature of the other relationship.

The Seven of Swords reversed can signify dirty politics or manipulation of the truth. It could be gaslighting, censorship, propaganda, smoke in mirrors, spinning, or distraction in order to avoid responsibility.

Activating the Seven of Swords

Trust is a funny concept. What we usually mean when we say that we trust someone is that we expect them to behave in a way that gives them responsibility for our well-being.

In this way, you're both controlling their behavior and you've also given them the power to hurt or disappoint you. A better approach is to trust that you can handle whatever life sends your way.

How can you trust your ability to respond to life?

SEVEN OF CUPS

Element: Water

Confusion, choice, potential, fantasy, dreams, imagination

Seven cups float in a mist. A figure stands with their back to us, looking at the cups. Each cup has something different in it - demons, riches, holy figures...

Dreaming and pondering the possibilities represented in the Seven of Cups is an essential part of the creative process. It's exciting to see all the potential. Without exploring, you can't know what's available to you and it can be difficult to choose.

Yet at some point, it is necessary to choose something. Otherwise, you can get overwhelmed. You could lose focus or get stymied and never actualize your dreams.

Maybe you're pondering a career change but aren't sure which path to choose. Maybe you want to go back to school, but aren't sure what to study. Or you're wondering if you should flip a house.

With the Seven of Cups, your ideas may be so up in the clouds, developed only in your imagination, that you need to separate what is real and what is not in order to make better choices. The Seven of Cups may tell you that you're ungrounded or entertaining an illusion.

One common interpretation of this card is a tendency to escape reality. It can represent any behavior used to numb such as drinking, smoking, drugs, gaming, social media, work, exercise, sex, reading... the list of ways to avoid your experience is endless. If escaping reality is habitual, it can signify potential for addiction, especially if the Devil card is nearby.

The person who draws this card may squander their resources by not choosing. Some choices in the cups look scary, but the key is to get out of the fog of fantasy, consider the possibilities, and then get into reality through choice.

Reversed Seven of Cups

Clarity, sobriety, choice, lack of imagination, limitation

When the Seven of Cups is reversed, it can be as if the mist obscuring the contents of the cups lifts and the options can be clearly seen. The Seven of Cups reversed can mean sobriety, seeing the truth, dealing with reality, and making decisions.

Maybe the 'Ooh la la!' of a new love interest is wearing off and you're finally seeing the person clearly and can now accurately assess whether to go deeper or to cut ties. Or perhaps you've realized that your career choice no longer suits you.

The Seven of Cups reversed can also mean a lack of choices. Maybe you want to go back to school but you're limiting your search because you're worried about time or money. Or maybe you've given up hope and aren't allowing yourself to dream.

Activating the Seven of Cups

Dreaming is an essential part of the creative process. There is magic in those cups. It's important not to yank yourself out of the creative reverie too soon.

Divine guidance can get muddied by the noise of conformity or pragmatism. There is a resonance which can feel like a pull inside when something feels true.

Can you remember decision points in your life when the mist cleared, and you knew with crystal clear clarity what your next step was?

SEVEN OF WANDS

Element: Fire

Standing your ground, boundaries, fierce commitment, dedication, challenges

A figure stands holding a wand in a protective pose. They wear mismatched shoes and defend against the six wands below. This is the same figure victoriously crowned with laurels in the Six of Wands card. Now the character has to defend the ground achieved by the win.

The struggle to maintain the higher ground gained by this character is the main point of this card. The Seven of Wands depicts the need to prove to yourself and to others that you're worthy and that you deserve your success.

This card can be the fallout after your promotion, with all of your jealous coworkers scrutinizing your performance. Or, this card can be as simple as sticking to your resolution to eat less sugar, despite the leftover birthday cake taunting you from the fridge.

The Seven of Wands can symbolize competing needs and not being pulled down into old, unsupportive patterns and habits. Depending on the cards surrounding it, this card can also mean going against the norm.

It could mean that you've chosen a different lifestyle than your friends and they are critical of you. Or perhaps your parents have different ideas about religion or the right way to raise children.

It can be lonely, but sometimes you have to fight for what you know is right, despite social discomfort and opposition.

Maybe you're the only one who has the courage to face your family's dysfunction. Or maybe you're the only one on the school board who thinks that funding for the arts is as important as funding for athletics.

Jesus is a famous example of someone who was teaching radical ideas at the time and who was crucified by his own people. While you're probably not the Messiah, there are plenty of times when you have to fight to maintain your sovereignty.

For any genuine change to occur, you need to fight the status quo, whether it is internal, external or both. Most innovative ideas are met with opposition and it takes strength, perseverance and courage to stand your ground.

Reversed Seven of Wands

Conflict-avoidance, need for social approval, falling into old patterns, compliance

Reversed, the Seven of Wands can mean you're not standing up for yourself. Maybe you're giving in to social pressure, not listening to your inner knowing, or are being intimidated by others.

I knew a woman who was a first generation Asian American who never stood up for herself when friends or family made racist comments. She told herself that she was protecting her kids, but instead she taught her children to be ashamed of their heritage and to avoid conflict.

The Seven of Wands reversed could represent feeling threatened by competition or lacking perseverance and follow-through. You could feel like your energy is pulled in multiple directions and you're having a hard time focusing and completing your projects.

Maybe you're wasting your time fighting for something that doesn't matter that much.

Maybe you just experienced an immense success, and you're having a hard time integrating the results. You could be sabotaging your success and losing the ground you worked so hard to gain. Maybe you're resting on your laurels instead of continuing to develop and grow.

When the Seven of Wands is reversed, it could represent that you're trying to keep the peace at the cost of your peace inside.

Activating the Seven of Wands

We all have a favorite way of sabotaging ourselves. Some people get busy. Some get sick or injured. Others go on a spending spree.

Success, love and money are magnifiers. When you experience more of them, be on alert for your favorite sabotaging strategies to come up and then don't take the bait. Stay in your body and breathe and you'll soon integrate the new, higher vibration of success.

What are some ways that you sabotage your success?

EIGHT

EIGHT IS a balanced number with a sound foundation. It's associated with success and business. The seed planted with the Ace has come to fruition and is ready to be harvested.

For the Pentacles, the Eight means their determination and commitment resulted in mastery. For the Swords, the Eight means an imprisonment formed by their anxious thoughts and limiting beliefs.

The Cups are finally rid of emotional baggage and are free to move forward in search of fulfillment. And the jubilant Wands release their pure energy out into the world.

EIGHT OF PENTACLES

Element: Earth

Work well done, skills, mastery, dedication, purposeful occupation

The character in the Eight of Pentacles is immersed in skilled work, having achieved mastery after the patient toil of the Seven of Pentacles. There is a village in the distance, showing that this work is a contribution to society. The eight pentacles show recognition and reward for work well done.

The health benefits of a sense of purpose in life are well documented. A sense of purpose is often expressed as the work that you do. When you have work that aligns with your interests, strengths, and values, you're more engaged. And if you're thriving in your sense of purpose, you're more likely to be thriving in life overall.

The person who draws this card is likely doing exactly what they set out to do and are doing it well. They're usually happy with their work and feel their efforts and results are appreciated.

If the Eight of Pentacles doesn't represent your work, it can mean another aspect of the physical plane, such as a healthy lifestyle. It could be a creative project that has come to fruition. Whatever it is, has likely taken a lot of concentrated effort and you feel pleased with the result.

Reversed Eight of Pentacles

Rat race, perfectionism, meaningless work, wasting time, unappreciated

Humans are wired to create and seek positive sources of meaning, such as purposeful work. When you lack positive sources of meaning, you can gravitate towards negative sources of meaning such as emotional, physical, financial, or relationship complaints.

The deceptively simple answer to many problems is to engage productively with the world in a way that transcends the self.

When the Eight of Pentacles is drawn reversed, it can represent the rat race. You may feel that your time is filled with meaningless busy work. It may mean you feel like a robot or a zombie in your job.

The Eight of Pentacles reversed can also show an avoidance of work through procrastination. There can be a lack of grounding and a general disconnection from the material world. It can mean sloppy work or an unwillingness to put in the work required for a desired outcome.

Sometimes, when the Eight of Pentacles is reversed, there can be the outer trappings of success, but with no internal sense of substance. You could be working to survive or to support a lifestyle rather than to live your life.

Maybe you're working hard, but for the wrong reasons or for the wrong cause. Maybe you think your value is connected to being productive and busy rather than from an intrinsic sense of self worth.

The Eight of Pentacles reversed can mean you aren't doing the work you're meant to do or you don't have the tools, time or support you need to do a good job.

Activating the Eight of Pentacles

Those who have accomplished mastery in their profession view their daily work as an expression of their soul.

What is the work you're meant to do?

EIGHT OF SWORDS

Element: Air

Trapped by limiting beliefs, victimhood, excuses, helplessness, negative thought patterns

The eight swords surrounding this figure are sharp and they demand change. In the Eight of Swords, the more you fight the change, the more uncomfortable it gets. In the Seven of Swords, the character is getting away with something, but now the character is caught and imprisoned.

The Eight of Swords can feel like being stuck in a negative situation with no way out. Fear and anxiety are likely in the driver's seat and there can be a sense of hopelessness. The Eight of Swords can signify feelings of isolation and the sense that no one understands.

The character depicted in the Eight of Swords doesn't want to look at the truth and acknowledge the changes that need to be made. If you drew this card, you may feel stuck in deeply entrenched patterns of negativity. You may have become blind to an alternative path to freedom.

Let's be real. This character could escape if they really tried. They could easily slip the binding and while those swords may be sharp, the circle isn't completely enclosing them. Plus, six of those swords are theirs from the boat.

The Eight of Swords illustrates how you can get trapped in your own story, or stuck in judgements and limited thinking, imprisoning yourself in your beliefs. There is a need to tap into deep inner strength and develop confidence in yourself. The answers to your problems are within reach.

It's easy to get attached to stories and overly identify with victimhood. I remember being in a healing workshop where a woman introduced herself as, "An Adult Child of an Alcoholic, an Incest Survivor, and an Insulin-Dependent Diabetic". The rest of us were only saying our first names, so it was a striking contrast.

She'd spent years in self-help groups and had developed her community and friendships based on her problems. She didn't know another way to relate. Her identity had become inseparable from her victim's stance. Someone in the group asked, "Do you have a name?"

Like the woman in the workshop, the folks who draw this card rarely recognize themselves in the card, so it can be a tough sell during a tarot consult. As a tarot reader, you'll likely see this card come up a lot because folks don't seek a tarot consultant when everything is peachy.

Guiding the person to understand that in most cases, their mentality is a big part of the problem, can help empower them to do the work that this card entails. This is the coworker who always has an excuse for not following through on time. Or the friend in a toxic work environment who can't see the patterns that are glaringly obvious to you.

Often, I'll turn it upside down and show the person for whom I'm reading how the blindfold and bindings fall off and how the character can then see clearly. They already have everything they need to be in charge of their life.

Like all the swords, there is mental anguish and unsupportive thinking that is harming the self and others. There may be deep ruts of learned helplessness habits. The person with this card is likely running abuse, control, sacrifice, lack, or addiction patterns and will continue to attract more of it until they can free themselves from their stories.

The abuse can be internalized, such as an eating disorder, self-criticism, or self-harm. Or the abuse can be externalized, such as struggling with money or authority figures.

Many times, the person who draws this card just needs to calm down and get some perspective. They are so triggered by the situation that they can't think clearly. The key to this card is to choose new thoughts, new behaviors, and a new story.

Reversed Eight of Swords

Breaking free, releasing limiting thoughts, better choices, a new narrative

When the Eight of Swords is reversed, the swords cut the ties and you can break free from limited thinking or from an oppressive situation. You become the witness in your life instead of caught up in stories.

It can signify burgeoning awareness and responsibility for your role in your suffering and the subsequent release of the distortion patterns that have been causing you to suffer.

Often when the Eight of Swords is reversed, it can mean that you're seeing how you have limited and oppressed yourself. It may still feel bleak, but there is hope because you have ownership of your situation, but in a detached and observant way.

Activating the Eight of Swords

The way out of the patterns of sacrifice, control and victimhood is to shift your focus. Victimhood requires a story. Try writing yourself a new story.

What is your new story?

EIGHT OF CUPS

Element: Water

Moving on, cutting your losses, breaking up, letting go, new path

The Eight of Cups card is set during an eclipse. The eclipse shows that the character is in a transformative process both internally (the moon) and externally (the sun). This person's emotions have been eclipsed and what was dear before no longer has a hold on their heart.

The figure has left behind the emotional stagnation and paralysis of the Five of Cups and traded the black cloak of the Five of Cups for a red cloak, symbolizing action.

The water recently crossed symbolizes that this person is leaving their past behind. The steep and jagged rocks show that the going may be up and down with loneliness and self-doubt to be overcome.

The person who has drawn this card has likely outgrown a situation. The self-discovery process of the Seven of Cups has brought them to the realization that something needs to change.

Maybe it was triggered by a loss or a betrayal, or maybe you hit a milestone birthday. When you draw the Eight of Cups, it can feel like suddenly you can no longer stand your situation or someone you're with.

Something woke you up to your dissatisfaction with your current situation and granted you the impetus to take the steps to become who you were meant to be. Whatever it takes.

There is still an element of grieving, but it is grieving in action. Putting one foot in front of the other, you're moving toward an improved reality.

Maybe you're sick and tired of taking care of everyone else all the time and need to take care of yourself. Maybe you lost yourself in a romantic relationship and don't even remember who you are anymore.

The Eight of Cups frequently accompanies a romantic breakup (often along with the Two of Cups or Lovers cards reversed and the Three of Swords). It shows up with a job change, moving, leaving a community, or other losses.

Maybe it's time to find a new job, end a relationship, help kids to leave the nest, close a business, or move to the country. It's hard to end something, but staying in an unhealthy situation, out of habit or comfort, can lead to more problems.

Once you kick the habit and wean yourself off of the familiar situation, you'll remember yourself and who you are.

It can feel lonely and isolating at first, making your way alone, but reclaiming yourself will create opportunities and fill the gap left for the ninth cup which symbolizes wholeness and fulfillment.

Reversed Eight of Cups

Regret, emotional baggage, not moving on, holding on to the past, fear of loss

When the Eight of Cups card is upside down, the stacked cups appear to follow the character and weigh them down.

The Eight of Cups reversed can mean not moving on and instead clinging to the past. There can be a lot of woulda, coulda, shoulda when the Eight of Cups is reversed.

It can mean emotional attachment, depression, or an emotional wound that hasn't healed. It can represent a denial of your dreams or an abdication of your truth. The Eight of Cups reversed can be the abandonment of your true self.

Less commonly, it can symbolize actual abandonment, perhaps experienced as a child and now projected onto your current relationships, which you cling to for fear of being abandoned again.

Sometimes the reversed, stacked, empty cups in the Eight of Cups can represent excess stuff that makes a home feel stagnant. Or the stacked cups could show an attachment to fantasy.

There may be an avoidance of commitment, such as running away from relationships or jobs when it gets Real. Look at the surrounding cards to see if there is avoidance or an addiction to numb the pain of staying stuck in an unhealthy situation. Regardless of the details, it's likely there is some emotional avoidance in operation.

Activating the Eight of Cups

The fear of loss can block you from going for it in life. Because we're in an illusion of separateness, we believe it is possible to lose something. As a result, we will hang on to what we have even if we don't want it because we're afraid of losing that thing we no longer desire or enjoy.

What do you need to release so that you can move forward with your life?

Eight of Wands

Element: Fire

Travel, launching, realization, things coming together, blast off

This is one of the few minor arcana cards that has no people in it. The Eight of Wands depicts eight wands that have been launched. There is a clear blue sky and conditions support the flight of the wands. The wands travel in unison toward their well-aimed destination.

Eight is the number of success and culmination, fulfillment and harvest. Since wands represent the element of fire, the Eight of Wands represents how you can share your fire or passion with the world.

The person drawing the Eight of Wands has paid their dues with the Seven of Wands where they fought to hold their ground. Their tenacity paid off and now they can direct their energy toward a goal.

The Eight of Wands is like being "in the zone" where you're focused and relaxed and feel you can accomplish anything.

The Eight of Wands card often symbolizes travel which is putting yourself out into the world. One client drew this card when she was flying to meet a long-distance love interest in person for the first time.

Another client drew this card when traveling back to his childhood home to sort out his parents' estate. The distance of the trip is irrelevant, it's the change in mindset and directing of intention toward fresh territory that the card is reflecting.

Whatever the endeavor, there is energy and momentum behind it, and if it is well directed, it should land well.

Reversed Eight of Wands

Backfiring, Delay, Misdirected, Misguided, Hesitation

The Eight of Wands reversed can signal a backfiring of plans. It's as if the wands fall out of the sky and onto the person who drew the card. It could signal that despite your best efforts, a plan isn't coming together.

Maybe a trip was canceled or postponed. I read for a client who planned to travel home for the holidays, and they drew this card reversed. I mentioned there may be possible delays or complications to their travel. A couple of days later, there was a big snowstorm that delayed all flights.

The Eight of Wands reversed can mean your energy is being misdirected and wasted. Such as the person who runs around doing tasks for others but nothing to support their own ambitions and is headed toward the burnout represented in the Nine of Wands.

There may be too much control because of underlying fear. Or there may be the fear of taking a risk and failing. It could represent reverse perfectionism, where the initiative is held back until it is "perfect," creating paralysis.

The Eight of Wands reversed could represent procrastination or holding back. It could mean that your energy is scattered in too many directions and, as a result, you can't seem to get anything accomplished.

Activating the Eight of Wands

Traveling forces you out of your normal context. Seeing an unfamiliar landscape or being in a different culture can bring new awareness. The Eight of Wands asks you to try yourself out in the world.

Where would you like to go?

NINE

NINE IS the last of the single digits and signifies a culmination. The beginning of the Aces has come to its ultimate expression. Like a rainbow, the number Nine incorporates the lessons of all the numbers.

For the Nines in tarot, each card takes it as far as it can and then completes the cycle. The Nine of Pentacles represents perfect balance with the material world. For the Cups, there is finally fulfillment and wholeness.

With the poor Swords, they are also coming to head with a dark night of the soul. And the Nine of Wands stands determinedly after a great exertion of will, defending their win and getting ready for the next challenge.

NINE OF PENTACLES

Element: Earth

Abundance, success, beauty, harmony, sensuality, flourishing

An elegant figure stands with poise and grace in a lush garden with ripened fruit. This is the same garden the Seven of Pentacles labored to tend.

The background of the Nine of Pentacles is yellow and there is a bird perched on their hand, symbolizing harmony with nature and spirituality. The character wears a yellow dress lined with red, showing a balance of spirit and passion.

Many of the elements of the Nine of Pentacles card are reminiscent of the Empress card. Flowers dot their gown, signifying fertility, beauty, and passion.

Two trees in the background frame the figure, an echo of the pillars of the High Priestess, the Hierophant, Justice, and the Moon cards which have been integrated. This person is fully in alignment with the element of earth.

The Nine of Pentacles is a success card. There are many ways to define success, and the Nine of Pentacles symbolizes the expanded definition of integrated earthly success.

Let's not forget the process the pentacles went through - from destitution and rebuilding through dedication and commitment. The state depicted by the Nine of Pentacles has been earned.

In order to stand in the garden in perfect harmony, the character on the card has likely surrendered their misperceptions about the true nature of security. They have surrendered the aspects of identity used as a false measure of self-worth. As a result, this person is fully present and engaged in their experience.

The person who pulls the Nine of Pentacles card upright may or may not have a huge bank account, but they will experience abundance. The Nine of Pentacles represents mature and whole success. This card denotes harmony with self, others, and with nature.

The Nine of Pentacles is not a climb to the top of the mountain and kick the competition's butt card. That's best left to the wands. This achievement didn't come from the reactionary strife and struggle like the Four of Pentacles. There was hard work, yes, but Nine of Pentacles is a card of having arrived, but not from racing to get there.

The Nine of Pentacles represents genuine success, where the person has relaxed into who they are and abundance is a natural byproduct of them living their truth and being in balance with life.

Reversed Nine of Pentacles

Striving, internal impoverishment, insecurity, unearned success, hollow achievements

Reversed, the Nine of Pentacles card can mean success that isn't integrated. Maybe you haven't learned your life lessons, or you've spent your money and energy unwisely on fancy blenders and expensive coffee drinks.

The Nine of Pentacles reversed can represent ill-gotten money by drug dealing, for example, or prostitution (literally or metaphorically selling one's self).

When I was in Kathmandu in 1999, I went to a restaurant with some friends in Bhaktapur Square. The restaurant was the nicest in the area, however; it was inexpensive relative to what a similar meal would cost in the United States. We're talking about an $80 meal costing $2, including a generous tip.

Everything on the menu was a la carte. One woman ordered a chicken dish traditionally served with rice, but didn't want to pay an extra five cents for the rice to go with it. She was so habituated to sacrificing in order to feel financially secure that she transferred her behavior into a setting where it made no sense.

When abundance isn't integrated, there will always be a feeling of lack regardless of the amount of money in your pocket.

With the Nine of Pentacles reversed, there may be disappointment with physicality, struggling with feelings of low self-worth and deservingness, rejection of your body, or feeling shame and disappointment about self image.

Maybe you aren't nourishing yourself with healthy food choices or you aren't stretching and moving your body. Your job could be stressful, or maybe you've developed an injury from working too hard.

There could be an illness that has you feeling as if your body is failing you. Or maybe the imbalance is represented by your finances or in the upkeep of your home.

Activating the Nine of Pentacles

Money comes from consciousness. The more you're anchored in the present time, the more you'll experience your naturally abundant state.

One way to become more physically anchored present in time is to experience your body as it is here and now. In body language, the hips and lower back are associated with abundance. Try standing up and doing nine hip circles in each direction.

What did you notice about how your experience shifted?

NINE OF SWORDS

Element: Air

Dark night of the soul, anxiety, breakdown, self-sabotage, monkey mind

A figure sits up in bed with her face in her hands. It's nighttime, and the background is black, with nine swords stacked horizontally in the background. The bed cover has a checkered print of roses alternating with astrological symbols. The bottom of the bed contains a frieze of two people fighting.

The Nine of Swords is what happens if you don't address the trauma and suffering symbolized in the Eight of Swords. The swords can become turned inward, and your thoughts can become disruptive.

The base of the bed symbolizes stored and suppressed memories. Swords represent thoughts and judgements that pull you out of present time and can cause suffering.

The key in this card is the bedspread. It can provide comfort to the existential suffering the person who drew this card is likely experiencing.

Things have come to a crisis point and the Nine of Swords can represent a dark night of the soul. We occasionally need these compressing nights of despair and questioning in order to break down and then break through to an empowered state.

The dark night can be an awakening experience, finally catapulting you beyond the stress, trauma, and limiting beliefs that have tormented you.

Maybe you're wracked with remorse and lay awake in bed, replaying events and beating yourself up. Or maybe you're worried about the future, running different scenarios, hoping to control an outcome.

One client got this card after she got engaged. Even though she was happy, she went into a tailspin, wondering if she'd made the right decision. Was she good enough? Was he good enough? Her doubts and fears haunted her, and she was overeating to numb herself.

Her previous relationship had been painful and although she'd healed and grown since then, it was still festering beneath the surface, and she was afraid to expose herself to being hurt again.

When she realized it was a healing surfacing in order for her to tolerate more intimacy, she reframed her response to the engagement as a detox and released her old story. Then, she could move forward and enjoy her life.

When the Nine of Swords shows up in a reading, your mind and emotions are not helping you. There are often deeper issues, such as unresolved traumas, informing the matter. The person who draws this card often nods because it looks exactly like how they feel and probably why they sought a tarot consultation.

When you're in a Nine of Swords moment, the best help can be to get some perspective. Now is the time to call a good friend or a therapist who can help you sort it out.

The good news is we all have access to the comfort and security the blanket represents. Viewing yourself from a universal perspective can remind you that you deserve to thrive. But you may need to address your shadow while also seeing the truth of your light beyond your shadow.

Reversed Nine of Swords

Clarity, relief, new perspective, opportunity to heal, avoidance, deep fear

The Nine of Swords reversed could show some relief from the mental anguish it portrays, possibly through therapy or from a new point of view.

Maybe you can see the crazy swirling of your thoughts, but you're witnessing it from a detached perspective. Or maybe you can see an addiction or abuse cycle more clearly and even though it sucks that you're in it, you can have awareness that it is just a cycle and that it will pass. Each time you get closer to releasing the spell.

On the other end of the spectrum, it could mean an intensification of the Nine of Swords. Maybe you're justifying your suffering or blaming others. Or maybe you're avoiding a necessary process.

Activating the Nine of Swords

The Nine of Swords can feel like a monkey is in charge of your thinking and is running around, throwing its feces on everything. Hang in there and try to allow yourself to be transformed by your experience. Try taking deep breaths. Connecting with nature can help ground you through this process.

What if your tormented state was a message from your higher self?

NINE OF CUPS

Element: Water

Happiness, fulfillment, satisfaction, completion, celebration

A figure sits wearing a red hat with two feathers signifying achievement. The character wears an expression of satisfaction. Behind him are nine cups displayed like trophies.

This is one of the happiest cards in the deck. Other decks call the Nine of Cups the "Wish Card" because it means that your dreams are coming true.

The Nine of Cups represents a culmination. It can represent the celebration of an achievement. Weddings, births, and graduations are associated with this card. It can represent any event where there is both success and emotional fulfillment.

In a relationship, the Nine of Cups can validate a deep connection with someone. It can feel like there's a base of friendship and mutuality already established. You may feel understood on many levels with sizzling chemistry. It can mean engagement or a deep level of commitment.

The Nine of Cups tells you it's time to enjoy the pleasures of life.

Reversed Nine of Cups

Emptiness, loss, disappointment, incompleteness, feeling of missing out

An upside down cup can't hold anything. When the Nine of Cups is reversed, it can symbolize a state of profound emptiness where happiness is sought externally through approval, achievements, or external appearances.

Maybe the person who drew the Nine of Cups reversed hasn't done their soul searching yet, or is clinging to something that is meaningless. Or maybe they are overindulging in food and drink. When the Nine of Cups is reversed, it can be a literal or metaphorical hangover.

There is a propensity for addiction with this card to fill the void. Drugs, alcohol, work, or sex could be used to cope with the inability to experience fulfillment.

Maybe the person who draws the Nine of Cups reversed achieved their dreams only to discover that it wasn't what they'd hoped for and they feel let-down.

Reversed, the Nine of Cups can also represent a lack of accomplishment. You could feel flat after realizing that you've wasted all of your effort on the wrong person, career or project.

A young client drew this card who was defining herself by caretaking and being overly responsible in her family in order to gain approval in a chaotic household. She felt profound remorse while watching her friends posting about all the fun and adventure they were having. Meanwhile, she was acting like she was 40 instead of 16.

Maybe you feel self-disgust but put on a cheerful face to cover up the truth. There can be a deep dissatisfaction with appearance, and emotional baggage blocking the ability to experience happiness.

Maybe there is difficulty receiving attention. It could be a feeling that nothing is good enough and a lack of appreciation and gratitude for what is. There can be a tailspin of negativity, focusing on what's wrong instead of giving attention to what is good.

You may not love yourself or feel you're worthy of love. Try to feel enjoyment in your life right now, even if it's just a little crumb. From there, it can grow.

Activating the Nine of Cups

Much of our cultural and religious programming tells us that pleasure is sinful. Many of us were raised to believe that the more you reject and control your passion and appetites, the more holy you are and the better off you'll be after you die.

Yet here we are on earth with our senses and drives. So how can we reconcile these oppositional viewpoints?

What if your physical experience is exactly perfect as it is?

NINE OF WANDS

Element: Fire

I'm still standing, perseverance, determination, boundaries, resilience

The character in the Nine of Wands has been in battle. They are wounded but still stand, temporarily resting, wary and on guard for the next round. The flat, gray ground upon which they stand reflects their determination to persevere.

Behind the figure are eight wands, each signifying an accomplishment and reminding them they've got the backing of their substantial experience. Behind the wands are green mountains. If only this character can get beyond the battle.

Upright this card means that you've almost reached the finish line but must face more tests of your moxie. You're likely exhausted from the struggle but must keep putting one foot in front of the other, drawing on your reserves of strength to power through to completion.

Maybe you're a sleep-deprived parent of young children. Or maybe all you have left to write is the bibliography of your final research paper. It could be an internal battle of limiting self-beliefs that leave you trapped, wounded, or defensive.

Perhaps you have poor boundaries and constantly need to defend yourself. Or possibly you have so many demands on your time and energy that you barely have time to go to the bathroom, let alone for self-care.

The Nine of Wands says, keep fighting. You got this, but you may need some major rest and recovery soon.

Reversed Nine of Wands

Depletion, hopeless, defeated, not a hill worth dying on, sacrifice

Reversed, the Nine of Wands could mean that you're exhausted from a battle that you can't win or shouldn't be fighting to begin with.

Maybe you feel like Sisyphus from Greek mythology, doomed to push a massive stone uphill only to have it roll back down again, over and over again for eternity. There is no sense of victory or achievement, only another endless load of laundry to fold.

There may be distortion patterns of struggle associated with this card and the belief that life has to be hard.

One client drew this card reversed in relation to his work. He came from a hardscrabble farming background and his interest in real estate investing was challenging his belief that making money required pain, sweat, and struggle. Because of his belief system, he had three side jobs, worked over 80 hours a week, yet could barely pay his bills.

He was exhausted from the struggle, but believed struggle was necessary to survive. Not only necessary but made you a better person and brought you closer to God. I suggested he observe other people who don't struggle to survive and observe if they were closer or farther from God and how he could be more like them. Within a year, he was down to two jobs, working 60 hours a week, with two investment properties.

The Nine of Wands reversed can suggest an addiction to cortisol, the stress hormone. Or positively, the Nine of Wands reversed could mean you're finally getting a break, and feeling a sense of relief or remission after a long struggle.

Activating the Nine of Wands

Many of us were socially conditioned to be pleasing and compliant, resulting in the sacrifice of ourselves, our lives, and often our truth.

This deeply embedded programming can cause you to say, "Yes" when you really don't want to. If you can't fully say, "No", then you also can't fully say "Yes."

What in your life do you want to say "No" to?

TEN

TEN IS the last number in the cycle of the minor arcana cards. Within the number Ten is the number One of a new beginning and the Zero of a cycle.

In tarot, Ten represents the outcome or fully realized energy of each suit. The four Tens in the minor arcana represent completion of the lessons in the suit and also the beginning of a new cycle.

The Pentacles show us the result of hard work and determination manifesting as success in the world. The Swords show how our thinking can cause our destruction if we don't learn how to discipline our minds.

The Cups illustrate a culmination of love and the Wands determinedly struggle through to completion.

TEN OF PENTACLES

Element: Earth

Culmination, success, status, community, wealth, generosity

The vantage point of the Ten of Pentacles card is looking from the inside out through an arch. A wealthy elder is petting their loyal hound.

The dog is reminiscent of the dog in the Fool card nipping at the Fool's heels, but now the dog is tame.

The elder wears a rich robe decorated with music and fruit, showing culture and wisdom. The walls are covered with crests and other signs of ancestry, lineage, nobility, achievement and social status.

There is a couple with a child beyond the arch, symbolizing the cycle of life. The couple appears to be happy and other structures in the background show upstanding society.

The Ten of Pentacles usually means good news in money related matters. This card could represent retirement or it could mean an inheritance coming your way.

Maybe your business is so successful that you are opening up another store. Or your presentation to your colleagues established you as an expert in your field.

The Ten of Pentacles represents a life well-lived. It is about leaving a legacy. It means you have accomplished something substantial. This card represents healthy security and multi-dimensional success in the material realm.

Reversed Ten of Pentacles

False security, keeping up with Joneses, setbacks, hyper-materialism

The Ten of Pentacles reversed can show a false sense of security or confusion about success, thinking that it comes from money, status, achievement, or recognition instead of from becoming more of who you're meant to be.

When the Ten of Pentacles is reversed, it can mean looking for external sources of validation or striving without ever being able to enjoy your achievements. Or it can mean that you're clinging too tightly to comfort and security and resisting your natural growth.

The Ten of Pentacles reversed can represent mismanagement of earth-related assets such as property, land, time, money, or your body. There may be an over-leveraged lifestyle in order to keep up appearances. Money that is supposed to come to you may be delayed.

It may be a good time to check in with your long-term goals. There may be a lack of preparation for the future, poor investments, or being short-sighted.

Awakening the Ten of Pentacles

There are many definitions of a life well-lived as there are humans.

What legacy do you want to leave?

TEN OF SWORDS

Element: Air

Rock bottom, defeat, failure, collapse, hope for a new beginning

A figure lies face down on the ground, stabbed in the back with ten swords. The figure wears a red mantle of unrealized dreams and the white sleeves of pure intentions.

There is darkness, stillness, and inevitability in the Ten of Swords. It looks like the figure never saw it coming. And the sword that went through the heart went in the deepest.

Calm water offers solace, and in the distance the sun rises over the blue mountains, representing access to wisdom and the opportunity to try again.

The only good news about this card is that the sun is rising. It's the conclusion of the dark night of the soul that was experienced in the Nine of Swords. This card represents the end of a long struggle. It most likely (hopefully) can't get worse?

Beginning with the Ace of Swords, you can see the theme of figures struggling to learn how to wield the sword's power appropriately. Each sword represents an opportunity to either understand or to misuse the weapon with the consequences of more guilt, regret, and complications.

Each misuse leads you farther away from experiencing the truth of your limitless self.

With all the back-stabbing, this card has a theme of betrayal. A betrayal of self or betrayal of the bigger truths about who you are. To get to this point, you have likely clung too tightly to your self-image and your self-definition.

You've probably looked for love, truth and success in the wrong places for the wrong reasons, and as a result, put your trust in the wrong people or institutions.

This card can represent the mind's role in creating disease in the body. Often we don't listen until there is a physical symptom that forces us to pay attention and change in order to be healthy. The swords are like bookmarks in our body of lessons that need to be learned and wounds that need to be healed in order to move forward without unconsciously repeating the same patterns.

The swords represent thinking and in the Ten of Swords; the mind has overridden instincts and you've destroyed yourself with your own attachment. This is the ultimate outcome of fear, stress, and negative thinking.

You've suffered. You're hurting. You're allowed to sob in the fetal position for a while. Once you can get out of the fetal position, go outside and look at the sky, or through a window if you can't get up off the floor. Think of yourself as just having come out of surgery and need to rest and eat soup. Be gentle with yourself.

As intense as the Ten of Swords looks, it is the end of a cycle and offers an opportunity for learning and to try again.

Reversed Ten of Swords

Reprieve, healing, survival, avoidance, relapse, despair

To understand this card reversed, it is helpful to imagine the swords falling out, signifying a respite from struggles. It can symbolize that recovery and healing has begun. Or that you have a new understanding about an old situation or pattern of behavior that was destructive.

When reversed, this card may not be as intense. It may mean having dodged a bullet. Or that a stressful situation is turning around and transforming.

The reversal can also mean avoidance or denial of completion and necessary ending, causing even more suffering.

Activating the Ten of Swords

As hard as it is, you've reached the bottom and there's nowhere to go but up. Time to let go and to move on. As you emerge from the abyss, try to use it as an opportunity to start fresh and choose mindfully what will serve you in your next life cycle.

How can you emerge?

TEN OF CUPS

Element: Water

Life is good, happily ever after, gratitude, harmony, magnanimity

The Ten of Cups card is like a brochure for happiness. Life is good, we're together, we have consummated our love, we have borne the fruit of our love.

A couple stands with their arms outstretched, looking up at a rainbow containing ten cups in its arch. They are close and connected. Two children play beside them. In the background is a home and gently sloping green hills with trees along a river.

This is one of the happiest cards of the minor arcana. The Ten of Cups is the ultimate culmination of love. It moves beyond the happiness and fulfillment represented in the Nine of Cups to an expanded and all-inclusive experience of love.

Despite the stereotypical image, the Ten of Cups card doesn't have to represent a romantic relationship. Maybe you went for a walk in the woods with your dog and saw a Pileated Woodpecker and felt grateful and in love with life.

It can mean you are happy at work and feel secure and appreciated. Or maybe your niece was just born and you're swelling with hope and love.

Reversed Ten of Cups

Unfulfilled, disharmony, jealousy, disappointment, dependency

When the Ten of Cups is reversed, it's like seeing the backstage of this idyllic scene. Maybe the honeymoon period is over and you absolutely cannot for one more minute stand listening to how your beloved chews.

As the cracks in a relationship begin to show, the emotions can either freeze or flood, and possibly a few cups will fly at each other. There may be a pulling apart and great distance in intimate relationships.

Maybe the relationship is over, but you don't have the wherewithal to move out and instead have to remain painfully suspended in limbo until the red tape gets sorted.

Or maybe secrets are being kept or revealed such as the front of the "perfect" family, when the reality is an active addiction which everyone enables.

When the Ten of Cups is reversed, there may be withholding of love and communication. Frozen emotions or major issues get swept under the carpet. There may be self-centeredness and a lack of compassion for others.

Feelings of being ostracized from your family or community are common. As are deep feelings of loneliness, disappointment, or like you're missing out.

The Ten of Cups reversed can have an illusionary aspect where the person who draws it has either been painfully relieved of their illusions, or else residing in a fantasy world. There may be sabotage of a healthy relationship in search of unrealistic relationships.

There is a strong sense of home with the Ten of Cups, so when it's reversed, it can mean homesickness, homelessness, or that your sense of home is in jeopardy.

Maybe the person who draws this card reversed skipped some lessons from the earlier cups, and is still stuck in the past or lacking self-knowledge or self-love, rendering them unable to function as an adult in healthy relationships.

Activating the Ten of Cups

It's easy to slip into an idealized future. It may feel safer, but then we delude ourselves and block the love that is available right now.

Our brain can form ruts of unhappiness through focusing on what is wrong instead of what is right. To get out of these ruts, it can be better to try for "good enough" than for perfect. Look for opportunities to experience more connection, beauty and goodness in the world, however small.

Where is the love in your life?

TEN OF WANDS

Element: Fire

Get 'er done, carrying burdens, overloaded, hard work, overextended

The character in this card awkwardly carries a heavy load of ten wands, as if walking uphill. Because this person's head is down, they can't see anything beyond the burden being carried. The character is moving toward the city in the background, bringing the wands to market.

This card suggests hard work and struggle, but with an end in sight. The Ten of Wands could signify the last stretch toward achieving a goal. Or it could mean that you're addicted to cortisol, the stress hormone.

The person who draws this card usually recognizes themselves as the character struggling to carry their burden. With the Ten of Wands, you have so much work to do that you get to the end of your day and realize you forgot to eat.

Maybe you don't know how you're going to pay child support this month. Or your deadline for your project is bearing down on you and you're nowhere near finished. Maybe you've over-committed yourself and are scrambling to keep your promises.

Maybe you're taking care of young children or ailing parents while working full time. Maybe your co-worker is on leave and you're carrying their workload, too.

Whatever the scenario, the person who draws this card likely feels overwhelmed. While an outsider would be incredulous that you are still standing, inside you may feel you could do more or should be able to manage better.

This can be an opportunity to show some kindness to yourself. The good news is that the ten is the end of the cycle, so hopefully you can rest soon.

Reversed Ten of Wands

Relief of burdens, giving up, purposeless struggle, overwhelm, martyrdom

The Ten of Wands, when reversed, can mean your burden has lightened. Or it can mean the other extreme, that there is no end in sight or you've dropped and scattered your load and now have even more work.

When this card is reversed, it can signal a tendency to struggle for struggle's sake. You know the person acting out this card when it's reversed, constantly running from one fire to another, never catching a break, their life full of craziness. It's exhausting just to hear about everything they've got going on.

Yet when you try to help them lighten their load, they just load up with more craziness. After some observation, you realize they will always have this level of craziness, because that's how they roll.

The Ten of Wands, when reversed, can feel like you have to do it all yourself. Perfectionism can complicate matters, feeling like it won't be done right if it's not done by you.

You may feel you're barely staying afloat, barely keeping your head above water, barely getting by. Or it can mean unfocused or distracted effort getting you nowhere, like the Red Queen in *Through the Looking Glass* who has to run hard in order to stay in place.

Activating the Ten of Wands

If you tend to over-commit and then feel unable to complete your tasks, or if you're too altruistic and neglect your self-care in order to help others, you may carry burdens that aren't yours.

How can lighten your load?

Court Cards

THE COURT CARDS are the pages, knights, queens and kings of the deck. They're considered minor arcana. Each of the court cards is associated with one of the four elements. The court cards usually represent a person.

All the pages as a group are associated with air. For example, even though the Page of Cups is in the suit associated with the element of water, because it's a page, it's considered both air and water. The knights are associated with fire, the queens with water, and the kings with earth.

The queens and kings can be an echo of an authority or influential figure in a family system such as a mother, father, grandparent or older sibling. The King of Pentacles reversed could represent your risk averse manager who recently shut your innovative idea down and can simultaneously represent your risk averse father.

Even though the queens and kings represent real people, they will echo shadow aspects of yourself to be reconciled. The real life people who the court cards represent may not even register as a big deal.

For example, a client drew the Queen of Wands reversed, and realized the card represented a woman she barely knew who was cheering inappropriately at her son's hockey game. This random mother made enough of an impression on her subconscious that she showed up in her reading as the Queen of Wands reversed. This extremely minor character in her real life triggered memories of her mother and illuminated her own fear of others perceiving her as socially inappropriate.

The knights usually represent a person, but not always. If they represent a person, it is likely a person in their 20s or 30s or someone older who feels or behaves like a young adult.

Often the knights can be interpreted as bringing more of the element they represent into the person's life. More love with the Knight of Cups, for example. Or a sound investment with the Knight of Pentacles. More energy or passion with the Knight of Wands and change with the Knight of Swords.

Many tarot systems correlate the court cards with an astrological sign. Capricorn for the King of Pentacles or Cancer for the Queen of Cups, for example. Don't get too hung up on the zodiac sign matching the court card. Sometimes it matches, sometimes it doesn't. It depends on what else is going on in the person's extended astrological chart and many other variables.

The court cards frequently don't match the gender, so it's wise to be careful with assumptions. It's also possible the same person will show up as a different court card depending on the context of the reading.

PAGES

The Pages usually represent children, and less commonly, pets. They can represent projects or news. The pages can also represent your inner child.

The Page of Swords often means going back to school or learning a new skill, for example, but it could also be your younger brother who is very smart.

If the page represents a child, it is usually a young kid up to the age of 22. However, if you're reading for the parent of an adult child, their adult child of any age may still show up for them as a page. It's also helpful to remember that chronological age doesn't always match up with the emotional or developmental age.

To complicate further, a niece, nephew or another child with whom there is a soul connection may show up in a reading and present as if it is the person's biological child.

Children incarnate to be with specific soul groups. If they can't get to their group through the traditional "womb door" as the Buddhists say, then they will find circuitous routes such as adoption, an aunt, a friend, or a neighbor.

One client drew the Page of Cups and the cards looked like a new child was coming into her life. She was already a grandmother and had a hysterectomy so a physical pregnancy wasn't possible. Sadly, a year later, her daughter died, and she adopted her granddaughter who was the child represented by the Page of Cups.

The pages, while associated with masculine or feminine consciousness based on their element (water and earth are feminine; fire and air are masculine), are not representative of a particular sex, but represent the essential qualities or nature of the child or endeavor.

As a tarot consultant, you may be asked to predict the sex of a child and my advice is to avoid any predictions, but especially on this topic. Parents may become attached to an outcome (for which you're now responsible) and it could adversely affect the baby, who may later feel like a disappointment for not fulfilling their parents' expectations.

Besides actual children, you can think of Pages like seeds, ideas, plans, or endeavors that are in utero or infancy. They can represent a strong possibility, about to be incarnated.

––––––––

PAGE OF PENTACLES

Elements: Air & Earth

Grounded, real estate, investments, building, business opportunity

A youthful figure dressed in a green tunic with a red hat holds up a pentacle. The green tunic symbolizes the connection with earth and growth, and the red hat symbolizes ambition.

If the Page of Pentacles represents a child, this child will express the earth-type traits. They may be physically and sensory oriented and may learn best kinesthetically. They may be athletic, interested in food, and appreciate beauty.

The child represented by the Page of Pentacles is often curious about how things work. This child may like Legos, robotics, or computer programming. They can be stubborn and set in their ways, craving the security of the familiar.

If this card doesn't represent an actual child, then it can mean goals are being set and plans are being set in motion.

With the suit of pentacles representing the earth element, the Page of Pentacles can represent any type of earthy topic such as money, real estate, or health. It is especially common when real estate is involved, such as making an offer on a property.

Maybe you're investing in a startup company. Or you're investing in your health with a new exercise program. If it's upright, it's likely a good investment.

REVERSED PAGE OF PENTACLES

Poor investment, unmotivated, risk-avoidant, perfectionism, stuck, bored

When the Page of Pentacles reversed represents a child, they may be unmotivated or lacking in ambition. They can lack self-discipline and have difficulty seeing projects through.

Or they may be overly concerned with money, status and power, willing to do whatever it takes to get it, regardless of who is hurt or what laws they break.

When the Page of Pentacles is out of balance, there may be possessiveness and feelings of lack leading to excessive accumulation. They could also slip into hedonism or overindulgence, lazing around on the sofa all day eating chips, watching shows, and spending other people's money.

Or they could be hyperactive, always moving and climbing, in order to render themselves physically present. Their senses may be so acute that they can't wear certain fabrics and the labels need to be cut out of all of their clothes. They may not want to be physically present so they space out or spend excessive amounts of time in fantasy or gaming.

Court cards associated with the element of earth can be less open to innovation and, when reversed, may be extra stubborn with a need to be right. Maybe they will only eat chicken fingers or foods that are white or orange.

When representing a goal or an undertaking, the reversed position can mean there will be delays and setbacks. Maybe they won't offer you the job. Your offer on the house may be rejected. Or your project could cost you more than you thought. Your endeavor could be stuck or not well-planned. Maybe there is a lack of drive and determination to bring the project or goal to maturity.

The reversed Page of Pentacles may show a lack of patience or a lack of focus. It could be something with the funding is off or the endeavor simply isn't viable, economically or otherwise. Or it could mean you're doing something for the wrong reasons.

Activating the Page of Pentacles

Science now confirms what we already intuitively knew - that playing in the dirt is good for you. The Page of Pentacles is asking you to till the soil and plant a seed. You might get dirty, but you'll be better for it.

What intention do you want to dig into?

––––––

Page of Swords

Element: Air

Training, plans, academics, intelligence, communication, new idea

A youthful figure in this card holds a sword and looks to the right. There are clouds behind the page and the wind blows the trees, symbolizing change and the potential for disharmony if the sword is not wielded wisely.

A flock of ten birds fly overhead signifying the ten cards of the cycle. The birds also represent the ability to use logic and reason to rise above any situation. There are mountains in the background, implying great wisdom is available on this path. The grass in front of the page looks bumpy and there is the intimation of a warrior who has the potential to break new ground.

The page wears red boots of action and ambition, but is the only page without a hat, simultaneously signifying open-mindedness, intellectual development, and also immature and underdeveloped judgment. The page's posture shows that the sword is a new tool they are learning how to use.

The Page of Swords is air of air, so when this card shows up there is mental activity and communication such as thinking, reason, communication, logic, and analysis.

If this card represents a child, this kid is smart and probably does well with their studies. This child is more oriented toward their mental body and intellectual development may come easily for them.

They may be bored and need more academic challenges than most. Ideas and new realms of thought challenge these kids. They may love to debate and can be quite brilliant in their observations.

If this card does not represent a child, it can represent learning a new skill or going back to school. Maybe you're being trained on some new computer software at work, or maybe you're starting a new job and have a steep learning curve for which you feel like the page, holding the sword trepidatiously but also eager to see what's possible.

REVERSED PAGE OF SWORDS

Manipulation, self-criticism, learning difficulties, blocked expression, impatience

When the Page of Swords is reversed, it is helpful to think of a sword not being used properly.

In an academic setting, the Page of Swords reversed child may struggle because of a learning disorder or an inability to focus. There may be a sense of mental overwhelm, not knowing where to aim the sword next.

Or there could be an overemphasis on intellectual development at the expense of the whole child.

For example, one boy in my daughter's 8th grade class went to college in order to be challenged in math, but his physical, emotional, and social skills were at a 6th grade level. While his test scores showed great intelligence, it wasn't an integrated intelligence.

There can also be a steep imbalance with the mental body and the child has become ungrounded or even disconnected from reality. Maybe there is too much time spent on screens and not enough time moving their body or in nature.

Other ways you can misuse the sword are by using sarcasm or communicating in a harsh, hurtful or inauthentic way. It could mean careless action without forethought. Or avoiding the sword altogether because of shyness and fear of your words being unwelcome.

If the page represents news or an opportunity and it is reversed, then it likely isn't good news or a good opportunity.

This card comes up a lot when considering a course of study. When the Page of Swords is reversed, it can mean the program of study isn't a good fit or it isn't the right time to pursue the study.

One woman for whom I read was considering going back to school for her PhD during an economic downturn. Logically, the PhD made sense, but for her, scurrying back to academia was an old pattern and an avoidance of living her life.

She would learn more from hiking the Himalayas or journaling about her dreams than anything academia could offer. She decided against the PhD and after a year of searching, ended up changing careers entirely, having a baby, and was much happier overall.

Activating the Page of Swords

Take a minute and check in with your mental, emotional, physical and spirit bodies. It's common to favor one body and to avoid the others.

Which body are you avoiding?

———

PAGE OF CUPS

Elements: Air & Water

Imagination, sensitivity, intuition, emotion, subconscious

The Page of Cups stands jauntily, gazing down at the cup in their right hand. A fish peeks over the side of the cup.

The page's tunic is adorned with red and white lotus flowers. In the background is water with gentle waves. The page wears a blue headdress showing connection with water in the mental sphere. The Page of Cups can connect with and access all the symbolic qualities of water.

Like the fish in the cup, the Page of Cups represents the sometimes surprising ways in which the unconscious can come to us. It may be through inspiration, intuition, dreams, or other forms that we can't understand.

If this card is a child, they are likely very sensitive. This kid is plugged in emotionally, intuitively, and spiritually. It may feel like this child can look right through you. The Page of Cups child can be intense and may process things emotionally.

Because of the unconscious aspects of water, this child often incarnates in order to heal deep, ancestral wounds and may have a lot of karma to process with family members.

If this card doesn't represent a child or a beloved pet, then the Page of Cups could represent a creative project. The project will probably have a divinely guided or channeled quality to it. For example, if the page represents writing a poem, the poem may feel like it is writing itself through you.

The Page of Cups could tell you to heed your inner calling and finally take the trip to Ireland. Or maybe it's reminding you to find a creative outlet. When the Page of Cups shows up, you may find yourself inspired to create something.

REVERSED PAGE OF CUPS

Hypersensitivity, shyness, blocked emotion, inability to cope with reality, psychic dumpster

Reversed, the world can simply seem like too much for these sensitive souls. This child or inner child can be fearful and emotional or have shut down and blocked emotions. Sleep issues, skin problems, allergies and digestive issues are common.

The key with this child is to help them learn to experience, express, and feel their feelings in a safe and constructive manner. Their emotions and sensitivity are their superpower and also their kryptonite.

Our culture and education system has a hard time understanding the way the Page of Cups child is wired and these institutions are often unfair and unable to support this child. They can be made to feel like their way of processing and operating in the world is wrong.

The danger, when reversed, is that the Page of Cups child could take on other people's energy or absorb the energy in the home, on the team, or in the room. The Page of Cups reversed may see ghosts, hear voices, or have vivid nightmares. Often, this child can be helped by strengthening their auric shield or psychic skin.

If this card represents a project but is reversed, then the project could lack soul and purpose. Maybe you're forcing something, something is stuck, or there is a lack of flow. It could mean hollow promises. Or there could be a block to receiving and allowing the project to come through.

ACTIVATING THE PAGE OF CUPS

Many of us were failed by our educational or familial systems and made wrong for feeling and understanding the world in a way that didn't fit into a tidy little box. Much of adulthood is about reclaiming your right to be who you are.

Are there any creative parts of yourself from childhood you would like to reclaim?

———

PAGE OF WANDS

Elements: Air & Fire

Inspiration, motivation, initiative, will, innovation

With the backdrop of a desert, the Page of Wands stands gazing at a wand and facing to the left. Salamanders decorate the yellow tunic, symbolizing the purifying power of fire. The red feather in their cap shows the ability to generate ideas.

The Page of Wands can represent an inspired project or initiative. It can also represent a quality you would like to experience or embody more. Maybe you just received the inspiration to write a screenplay. Or maybe you're learning how to play pickleball.

Fire can also purify and prompt initiative such as writing a letter to the Superintendent of your school because the Athletic Director is giving an unfair advantage to some kids while other kids get left out. Maybe you're feeling fired up to throw out a bunch of old journals containing pages lamenting the loss of your ex-girlfriend who you now realize was actually quite mean to you.

As with all the pages, the Page of Wands can represent your inner child or an actual child. As an actual child, this kid is fiery with some sass and a lot of energy.

The child may be argumentative, rebellious, or mischievous, but also clever, playful, and funny. They may express their energy physically and athleticism is common.

The Page of Wands child wants to express their fire and loves their place in the center of attention. They're charismatic, daring and enjoy taking risks and healthy competition.

REVERSED PAGE OF WANDS

Bossy, undirected energy, difficulty focusing, bragging, rebellion

If the Page of Wands reversed represents a child, they may have difficulty managing their fire and energy, particularly the emotion of anger, and they can act like a bully or a tyrant. They may be overly willful or self-oriented.

If lacking a strong authority figure or clear parent-child boundary, the Page of Wands child may decide, as the strongest personality in the family, that they should be in charge and will take over the household, controlling with their moodiness, rage, and need for attention.

Particularly if they're insecurely attached, this child may feel compelled to be the center of attention. They may also be prone to exaggeration or need to win at all costs.

This card can show up when kids have difficulty focusing or completing tasks and may have attention issues or oppositional defiance which can also be thought of as unintegrated or ungrounded fire. When these children have an idea, they can move straight to action without considering the risks.

Conversely, when fire is out of balance, the child may be disconnected from their will and feel stuck and unable to start projects. Or they start multiple projects, but lack the drive and follow through to complete. Sometimes these kids can burn themselves out with all of their fire.

Spirited kids get shut down a lot, especially in a traditional school setting where they were likely told to be quiet and to sit still and to pay attention. The Page of Wands child may struggle in traditional school settings and often learns by doing and through movement and engagement rather than by a placid receiving and regurgitation of information.

If the Page of Wands reversed represents a project, it could mean there's not enough energy or inspiration to carry it through. Or it could mean your energy is misdirected, such as a business idea that's based on competition rather than authentic passion.

If you have a great idea, but you haven't been able to fire it up, The Page of Wands reversed could tell you to just get going already.

ACTIVATING THE PAGE OF WANDS

Unfortunately, it usually isn't the highest quality work or the most talented artists who become famous. It's the ones who are the most ostentatious.

Maybe you don't want to be famous, but it would be nice if others could benefit from your genius, right?

What are some ways you could share your unique genius?

KNIGHTS

The Knights, as a group, represent the element of fire. The Knights are the Pages who have come of age and now hunger for a quest aligning with their governing sign and element. They represent a person, influence, or opportunity coming into your life.

If the Knight represents a real person, then they will often be in their teens to 30s. However, I've seen 40- and 50-year-olds present as a Knight in a reading.

Each Knight wears a suit of armor and is ready for battle, ready to fight for their respective element. When upright, they bring more of the element they represent into your life. When reversed, they take the element out of your life.

The Knight of Pentacles brings fire to the earth element such as financial opportunities, jobs, money, land, or health. The Knight of Swords adds fire to air and charges into our lives with an explosion, demanding change and action.

The Knight of Cups fires up the element of water, bringing more love into or out of your life. And the fiery Knight of Wands brings energy, passion and vitality into or out of your life.

––––––

KNIGHT OF PENTACLES

Elements: Fire & Earth

Pragmatic, ambitious, hard-working, business, investment

The Knight of Pentacles sits on a strong black horse who stands still. The knight's plume is green and resembles oak leaves, a nod to Druidic and pagan traditions, and also showing a connection with nature and growth.

In the background, the fertile fields are plowed and ready to be planted with the seed the Knight of Pentacles offers. There are green mountains beyond symbolizing achievement. The knight wears a red tunic and the braiding and bridle on his horse are also red, signifying strength and ambition.

The Knight of Pentacles brings the element of earth into your life. If it is upright, perhaps a new job or a real estate investment is coming your way. Whatever it is, you're being offered an opportunity for growth in the material realm such as financial, physical, land, food, or commerce.

The Knight of Pentacles represents ambition, tenacity, patience, responsibility, and hard work. If this knight rides into your reading, you may need more of these traits applied in your life. It could mean adopting a healthy lifestyle or exercising more fiscal responsibility. The Knight of Pentacles is in it for the long haul, and reminds us practice, patience and stamina are key ingredients for a successful outcome.

If the Knight of Pentacles shows up in a relationship reading, it likely represents a down-to-earth type of relationship with a slow burn, meaning it would be best to take it slow and steady. It could also represent an investment in a partnership, such as marriage.

The Knight of Pentacles is the most loyal and committed of the knights. The relationship may not feel like the romantic passion of the Knight of Cups, nor the burning chemistry of the Knight of Wands. However, their earthy sensuality is built to last.

Reversed Knight of Pentacles

Poor investment, holding back, lack, stuck, loss, limitation

When the Knight of Pentacles is overturned, the fields lie fallow. There can be a lack of motivation, wanting all the nice things money can buy but without the willingness and determination to go work for it.

The Knight of Pentacles reversed can warn of a poor investment of resources, whether it is money, time, or physical work. It could symbolize a blocked or dead end opportunity such as a deal not coming to fruition.

Depending on the other cards surrounding the reversed Knight of Pentacles, there may be issues with gambling or deal-chasing. When the Knight of Pentacles is out of balance, there could be tendencies toward workaholism, greed, cheapness, or possessiveness. There may also be a lack of ambition, lack of focus, and not taking responsibility.

Sometimes the person who draws this card may unconsciously seek a parent-type figure in a romantic partnership to take care of them financially and otherwise.

Some caution and skepticism is in order when this knight is reversed. It could represent a buyer beware situation, such as purchasing a car that's a lemon. Be sure to double-check the bid from the contractor and read the fine print on your legal documents.

Conversely, there could be too much caution, control, clinging to limited ideas of right and wrong, and black and white thinking.

Activating the Knight of Pentacles

The Knight of Pentacles can be your best ally when you want to invest in a goal, especially if it is long term or challenging.

Is there any area of your life calling for more practice, patience, or stamina?

———

KNIGHT OF SWORDS

Elements: Fire & Air

Change, action, decision, impatience, communication

A knight with a sword raised charges into battle. In the background, the strong wind bends the trees and the birds are struggling in the wind. The clouds are harsh and jagged, the same type of clouds in the battle portrayed in the Five of Swords.

The gray horse is running, and there is a sense of urgency. The knight has an expression of fierceness and determination. Red plumes fly behind them, signifying an idea or ambition for which they will fight. They are armored and their cape is decorated with birds and butterflies, emphasizing their connection to transformation.

The Knight of Swords brings fire to light up the air in your life. This knight charges into your life and demands action. If you can make the Knight of Swords your ally, you can experience their transformative power. It may be an unwelcome change, but a necessary change for your highest good.

The change the Knight of Swords represents can take many forms. Maybe they are reorganizing your work group. Maybe it's a wake-up call with your health. I drew this card when I collided with a deer. The deer ran off, but my car was damaged. The insurance paid for a rental car which allowed me and my daughters to attend a funeral in Texas for my beloved uncle.

If the Knight is charging into your life romantically, prepare for stimulating intellectual discussions and adventure. The person represented by the Knight of Swords won't waste your time with games. They may not be as sentimental as the Knight of Cups, but the communication will be electric and sincere.

If the Knight doesn't represent a person, then it may mean you have to take some decisive action in your life before it is taken for you.

REVERSED KNIGHT OF SWORDS

Haste, heedlessness, avoidance of change, indecision, confusion

Two helpful ways to think about the Knight of Swords reversed are, one, like too much air coming into your life, like a tornado. Or two, not enough air, like a sailboat with no wind.

The tornado could feel like the Universe kicking your butt with a needed change in order to wake you up, since you weren't doing it consciously. An excess of air could look like avoidance of taking action, such as indecision or analysis paralysis.

The reversed knight can show scattered, unfocused energy, such as giving your time to an unworthy cause. You may have lost your gumption and drive and possibly even forgotten what you were so excited about. There can be a lot of reactivity when this card is reversed, choosing actions based on what you don't want rather than what you do want.

Like the tornado, a reversed knight can also show ruthless ambition, impatience, impulsiveness, or heedlessness. Possibly with no consideration of consequences nor the impact on others.

ACTIVATING THE KNIGHT OF SWORDS

If the Knight of Swords is presenting itself in your life, it's best to direct the energy if you have any choice in the matter. Like a triple espresso, this energy can be harnessed when you need some drive to make change. Just make sure you're clear with your intention and that you're "fighting" for the right thing.

What change are you willing to fight for?

KNIGHT OF CUPS

Elements: Fire & Water

Love, romance, sensitivity, intimacy, support, intuition

Love flows everywhere the Knight of Cups rides. This card represents an awakening of the heart, allowing more love to flow in.

A knight on a gentle steed offers a cup. Their horse is calm and appears to know the formal art of dressage. Water flows in the background, symbolizing passion and the emotions.

There are wings on the Knight of Cups like Hermes, the messenger of the gods, and the fish from the Page of Cups now decorates their tunic, showing they have now incorporated the ability to engage with the unconscious and bravely communicate feelings.

The love the Knight of Cups represents could be passionate, such as a weekend getaway with your lover. Or it could symbolize a potential love interest, such as the guy you talked to at your high school reunion who you can't stop thinking about.

The Knight of Cups could show warm familial connections, such as your brother flying in and your family being together for a holiday. Or spending the day at the science museum with your grandchild and being present with them as they explore the world.

Maybe you are edging back out into the world after being isolated because of a loss and are feeling understood and accepted by your community. Perhaps a therapist or friend has seen your pain and was lovingly present for you in your suffering. Or maybe your long-term relationship was revived after some vulnerable conversations.

The Knight of Cups can represent any type of love coming into your life. Look to the surrounding cards to understand the context in which the Knight is being received.

REVERSED KNIGHT OF CUPS

Losing love, shame, pushing love away, illusion, attachment

When the Knight of Cups is reversed, it symbolizes love going out of your life. You may have lost that loving feeling for someone. Or maybe you've slipped into mania and obsession about the attractive person at the gym and it has now become more about your mental health than about love.

Maybe someone you considered a good friend has betrayed you. Or, perhaps you've forgotten the love in your committed partnership and you've become roommates on auto-pilot.

Like all the knights, the Knight of Cups is fire and the suit of cups represents the element of water. When water and fire are in harmony, there is a perfect balance, but when it is out of balance, there are uncontrolled emotions, hyper-emotionality, fantasy, or vampirism.

Like all the cups, your emotions may need to be recalibrated. The reversed Knight of Cups can mean either frozen emotions or flooding emotions leaking out on everyone around you. Reactions may be disproportionate to the actual event because you're responding to something deeper and older that the current situation is triggering.

When reversed, the Knight of Cups could activate the shadow aspects of love. Maybe you're crushing hard and obsessing about the object of your affection, using it like a drug. Or maybe you're in a toxic relationship, but you can't seem to let go. Maybe you're stalking someone or being stalked.

There can be a deficit of self-care and self-love. Maybe your abandonment issues are fully activated and you're drowning your sorrows in chardonnay, or looking for love in the bottom of a pint of double chocolate ice cream.

The reversed Knight of Cups can also suggest a projected fantasy or that your emotions are being toyed with. Perhaps you're being manipulated, or perhaps you're the one manipulating.

A common scenario with the Knight of Cups reversed is vampirism. Often, an empathic person is dealing with someone who is narcissistic, addicted, or both, and they are mired in a role of rescuing. The partner, friend, adult child, coworker, or boss may be sucking their life energy.

One client got this card every time her boyfriend came into town. The cards surrounding the Knight of Cups never looked good - the Seven of Swords, Queen of Pentacles reversed (his mother) and the Devil card. But he was so charming and she couldn't see the situation clearly because her alcoholic father never gave her the love and attention she needed as a child.

For a painfully long time, she could only see her wounded child's version of the knight. She perceived her knight coming to her, but the water, in her case, represented projection, illusion, and emotional manipulation. Eventually, she realized he was lying to her while she was footing the bill for him.

After enough time passed with nothing changing and she'd lost a substantial amount of money to him, she saw the chinks in the armor and he fell off his horse with a painful plop.

ACTIVATING THE KNIGHT OF CUPS

The Knight of Cups offers love. The question is, can you receive it? Opening your heart requires courage. Raw, authentic communication from the heart creates safety and allows for more love to be experienced.

If you're feeling stuck in a relationship, start speaking your heart's truth.

What I am most afraid to say is...

———

KNIGHT OF WANDS

Element: Fire

Action, initiation, adventure, challenge, libido, go time!

The Knight of Wands is facing to the right, signifying action. The knight's plume resembles flames and the knight's tunic is decorated with salamanders, considered fire spirits that can both create and put out flames. In the background is a desert scene with three pyramids. The horse rears as the knight seeks a challenge.

This card can represent passion, momentum, and straight up energy. If this card has ridden into your reading, you already have the drive and fire you need to get yourself going. The Knight of Wands is an action card. This knight knows how to make things happen.

The Knight of Wands does not like to sit around. They like freedom, action, and exploration and tell you to do the same.

The Knight of Wands can give you the explosive power you need to birth, to breakthrough, or to launch an initiative. The Knight of Wands accepts no excuses. There are no reservations and no regrets.

In a relationship reading, the Knight of Wands can show sizzling chemistry, depending on the surrounding cards.

If the Knight represents an actual person, they are dynamic and exciting. They will often be the life of the party.

There may be some restlessness with the Knight of Wands and an inability to commit when there are so many adventures and the entire world to explore.

REVERSED KNIGHT OF WANDS

Lack of focus, no drive, unproductive, frustration, rebellion, adrenaline junkie

Reversed, the Knight of Wands can mean you have low energy or your energy is unfocused or scattered. Maybe you're being overly harsh and critical of yourself. Or there could be unprocessed anger coming out sideways, scorching those nearby.

There may be over-competitiveness, bragging or extremism. With the intense fire and drive, the knight can be impatient, disruptive, or even hyperactive and have a hard time completing projects and instead moving on to the next exciting endeavor.

The reversed Knight of Wands could warn of rushing into something. Conversely, it could mean you're stuck or holding back, squelching your drive and ambition.

ACTIVATING THE KNIGHT OF WANDS

The Knight of Wands asks you to get in the driver's seat of your life and take off the emergency brake. You may not know where you're going and that's the fun of it.

How can you be more adventurous?

QUEENS

All the queens in tarot are the element of water. The Queen of Pentacles is water of earth, the Queen of Swords is water of air, the Queen of Cups is water of water, and the Queen of Wands is water of fire.

Like the kings, the queens can represent both actual people and mirror an aspect of the person who draws the card. Queens can represent relationships with a parent or parent figure.

QUEEN OF PENTACLES

Element: Water & Earth

Nurturing, practical, sensual, executive, wealth, achievement

The Queen of Pentacles sits facing to the left, the side of feminine aspects of consciousness, and gazing down at the pentacle in their lap like a baby. The queen wears red and green with two small feathers in a closed crown and is framed with flowering vines. Growing around their throne are flowers in the fertile soil.

On the arm of the throne is a goat, a nod to the astrological earth sign of Capricorn. The back of the queen's throne is decorated with fruit, signifying abundance. The cherub at the top symbolizes parenthood. A rabbit in the right-hand corner of the card shows this card's correlation with fertility.

The Queen of Pentacles is the abundance of earth incarnate. With this queen, all physical and security needs are met. This queen has the highest thread count sheets on their bed and if they have kids, they are never hungry. The Queen of Pentacles can both totally rule and rock the domestic scene, the bedroom, and be a successful entrepreneur or partner at their law firm.

In their relationships, they are loyal and committed, often preferring conventional arrangements.

The Queen of Pentacles appreciates quality, and their surroundings are beautiful. This queen likely has a green thumb or at least an appreciation of nature and pets who adore them.

The Queen of Pentacles craves security and comfort in all aspects of her life. They are hard-working, ambitious, organized and an upstanding citizen, respecting society's values and norms. As an earth sign, they are deeply sensual and usually love physicality, sexuality, and food.

REVERSED QUEEN OF PENTACLES

Rigid, controlling, risk avoidant, dogmatic, status-seeking

Like mud, when reversed, The Queen of Pentacles could be insecure, codependent, merging with others, or stuck and refusing to take responsibility for their life.

Their identity may be so wrapped up in their children or their partner that they have no center in themselves. This could look like martyrdom, jealousy, victimhood, addiction, caretaking, or enabling.

There can be a lot of fear, symbolized by the rabbit, when this card is reversed. And like a rabbit, they may freeze or run in the face of danger.

When the Queen of Pentacles is reversed, they could be rigid like a rock and close-minded with their religious or conventional mainstream beliefs about what is "right".

They may prefer compliance and obedience and may be controlling. There may be scarcity consciousness and limited ideas about money. They may be risk averse, preferring the comfort of maintaining the status quo.

When reversed, The Queen of Pentacles can feel smothering and can cripple their children by keeping them dependent on her. They can block their growth with their fear, encouraging them to avoid risks and to opt for safety instead of exploring the world.

The Queen of Pentacles reversed may also be overly concerned with social acceptance and can discourage their kids from being original or outside of the norm. They may micromanage friendships, activities, or appearances in order to maintain what they consider an appropriate veneer.

When reversed, there is an imbalance of earth which can look like issues involving the body, such as hypochondria, germs, eating disorders, shame, being overweight, or being overly concerned with appearance.

Or the imbalance could manifest as issues involving security, such as financial issues, or relationship issues. They may overcompensate for their insecurity and lack of grounding by accumulating material possessions.

ACTIVATING THE QUEEN OF PENTACLES

Feeling safe, grounded, and nurtured are the specialties of the Queen of Pentacles. If your primary caregiver wasn't the greatest at providing these qualities, then your inner child may still seek them.

How can you nurture yourself?

––––––

QUEEN OF SWORDS

Elements: Water & Air

Wise, fair, logical, integrity, clear communication

The Queen of Swords faces to the right on a throne adorned with a butterfly and a cherub symbolizing the transformative power of air. Clouds, the product of water and air, form behind them and there is wind in the trees.

A bird soars overhead, showing higher knowledge, freedom, ideas, and spirituality. The bird also shows an ability to remain in control of emotions. There are clouds on their robe and behind them is a river.

The person represented by this card is likely drawn toward analytical or technological pursuits. With the watery nature of all the queens, the Queen of Swords is in touch with their emotions which temper their rational approach.

The Queen of Swords can be witty, and verbal banter is a specialty. They love with their mind first. For your anniversary, this queen may write you a poem in the style of Dr. Seuss that is as touching as it is hilarious.

The Queen of Swords uses their intellect to cut through the noise directly to the truth. This is the lawyer you want representing you or the doctor researching the cure for cancer. They approach life head first, but their intelligence is integrated with their heart.

REVERSED QUEEN OF SWORDS

Cold, harsh, critical, aloof, close-minded

The Queen of Swords reversed can be like an ice queen. They may live mostly in their mind at the expense of their emotions and physical body.

There may be a no-nonsense approach to their parenting. The emphasis and measurement of a child's success may be academic scores or athletic achievement. Early childhood may be challenging since the Queen of Sword's favorite way of connecting is through the intellect.

Children with a reversed Queen of Swords parent may have had their emotions rationalized away or could feel wrenched out of the reveries of childhood prematurely in the pursuit of accelerated reading or math.

With a reversed sword, they may feel harshly criticized. Ideas are valued, but the creative process, emotional intelligence, and imagination may not be valued.

When any of the court cards are reversed, there is a misuse and misapplication of the element. With swords representing air and the mind, it may appear as argumentative, judgmental, self-critical, or guarded.

ACTIVATING THE QUEEN OF SWORDS

The Queen of Swords is an excellent strategist. They can help you cut through the clouds of stories in order to achieve a fair outcome. This queen reminds you it's your life and you get to decide.

Is there any situation where cutting through emotional attachment would help you respond more clearly?

———

QUEEN OF CUPS

Element: Water

Nurturing, comforting, adaptable, psychic abilities, empathic

The Queen sits holding a cup, facing to the left with water surrounding them. They wear a flowing gown of blue, symbolizing their connection to the element of water. Cherubs decorate their throne, showing fertility and creativity. The top of their throne resembles an oyster shell, a nod to the goddess Aphrodite.

Because the dominant culture in the United States does not value many of the Queen of Cups' strengths and qualities, they may not get fair credit for their unquantifiable contributions and may feel unsuccessful. Later in life, they usually get over it and embrace their way as their superpower, but it can be painful until they do.

The Queen of Cups is tuned in. They can pick up on the subtleties and the undercurrents of situations. When they sense something is "off" you'd do well to heed the hunch. They will somehow call you at the exact moment when you just lost your job and need someone to talk to. They will listen and comfort you when you're upset.

Because of their deeply intuitive nature, they often have a vibrant dream life and can be connected with lunar cycles and with the spirit world. Because of their sensitivity, they have the unique ability to put their finger on the pulse of the moment and can often accurately predict trends and events.

The Queen of Cups is loving and nurturing, as well as creative. As a parent, they may enter imagined worlds right along with their children.

While often in leadership roles, the person represented by the Queen of Cups may struggle to avoid being cast in a supporting role because they can be so darn supportive. As the element of water, they can morph into whatever container they are put into. This is their greatest strength, but also the greatest source of suffering.

REVERSED QUEEN OF CUPS

Lack of identity, codependency, hypersensitivity, overly emotional or suppression of emotions, martyrdom

When the Queen of Cups is reversed, there can be a danger of losing their sense of self, leading to codependency and enmeshment.

With the Queen of Cup's highly developed sensitivity, they may absorb the negative emotions or toxic energy of their environment. As a result, they may need to strengthen their auric shield. Excess weight is a common way to mitigate the over-sensitivity and lack of boundaries in order to create a physical buffer.

Conversely, they can be manipulative or vindictive, controlling others with their emotions. They may seek power in passive-aggressive ways. Or they could be attached to victimhood, always seeking sympathy.

The Queen of Cups reversed may present as needy and clingy, with the potential to be vampiric. There may be addiction, manipulation, hypersensitivity, depression, enabling, or too much caretaking.

More than the other three queens, the Queen of Cups, when reversed, can be a smothering parent, prone to enmeshment with their kids. Like the Queen of Pentacles, they may unconsciously stake their identity and self-worth on being a parent and live through their children.

The Queen of Cups reversed parent may appear to be extremely loving, so it's difficult to identify the energetic truth underneath the affectionate behavior that is crippling their child by making the child their source instead of allowing the child to live their own life.

Boundaries can become blurred and confusing, with the child becoming too close to the parent or energetically and emotionally replacing the other adult parent. This form of triangulation is common and while subtle, can lead to many other problems.

ACTIVATING THE QUEEN OF CUPS

It's easy to feel overwhelmed by emotions, but emotions can be a powerful tool for awakening. Jealousy, for example, can be harnessed to clarify your desires, and anger tells you that your boundaries have been violated and spur you to make a change.

Usually, there are emotions you prefer to avoid. The emotions you dislike will help you awaken the most if you allow yourself to experience them.

What emotion do you prefer to avoid? What would happen if you didn't avoid it?

———

QUEEN OF WANDS

Elements: Water & Fire

Witchy, dramatic, competitive, dynamic, adventurous

The Queen of Wands faces forward, but looks slightly to the left, showing an openness to emotion and intuition. Lions adorn their throne and there is a desert scene behind them.

They are clothed in yellow and hold a blooming sunflower like a scepter in their left hand. There is a black cat at their feet, reminiscent of a familiar in witchcraft.

Sunflowers follow the sun and symbolize a healthy expression of the solar aspects of the self. In flower essence therapy, the sunflower remedy correlates with the solar plexus area which is associated with issues of personal power and a balanced ego.

The Queen of Wands knows how to make things happen. They may have a dramatic flair in the way they dress, communicate, or in their lifestyle.

Athleticism may come naturally to them and they likely played sports and were a leader of their student body.

As a parent, the Queen of Wands focuses their vibrancy on their children, who bask and grow in their light. The Queen of Wands is playful and will support their children to go for their goals. They will provide whatever the kids need to compete and to be successful.

The Queen of Wands enjoys challenges and competition. Like a lion, they can be fierce and will fight for what they believe in.

Reversed Queen of Wands

Controlling, arrogant, selfish, jealous, misdirected ambition

When the Queen of Wands is reversed, there can be self-aggrandizement, arrogance, and selfishness. They may stare at themselves in the mirror all day and expect you to give them all of your attention, too.

All the queens and kings have the capacity for narcissism when reversed, but the King and Queen of Wands seem to be the most susceptible to self-absorption, often upstaging their children in order to feed their imbalanced psychological state.

When the Queen of Wands is reversed, they feel insecure and not good enough. As a coping mechanism, they may overcompensate by demanding attention in unhealthy ways, such as being sick.

The Queen of Wands may be overly concerned with appearance. Or, like the queen in Snow White, they may perceive their children as competition for attention.

There can be a strong need to control, and compulsive tendencies may be present. If the person represented by this card is more reserved, then there may be nervous energy and anxiety.

When the Queen of Wands is reversed as a parent, you probably didn't see them much and may have felt like they didn't see you. You may have been left alone or with babysitters a lot and felt like you were an inconvenience to the queen's social life.

You may have felt like an accessory to their wardrobe or that they cared more about other people's opinions than they did about your opinions.

The reversed queen may have put themself and their needs before their children and family, possibly in a passive-aggressive way such as martyrdom or illness

A client's mother who exemplified the Queen of Wands reversed deliberately scheduled an optional medical procedure while my client's family planned to take a long-overdue family vacation. He didn't buy into the drama and went on vacation, leaving the reversed queen to find another audience for her antics.

Repressed anger is common from being conditioned to be nice and accommodating. Here, the Queen of Wand's fire may be misdirected as resentment, demanding, and self-righteous.

ACTIVATING THE QUEEN OF WANDS

The Queen of Wands is a natural leader. No one messes with this queen. Invoke their moxie when you need to kick some butt.

Is there any area of your life where you would like more sovereignty?

KINGS

All the kings are associated with the element of earth. Each king is a matured version of the element they represent. The King of Pentacles doubles down on the earth element as both a king and as a pentacle. The King of Swords is earth of air, the King of Cups is earth of water, and the King of Wands is earth of fire.

Like the queens, the kings can represent both actual people and shadow aspects of the self. The kings also represent a parent.

———

KING OF PENTACLES

Element: Earth

Wealth, prestige, pragmatic, success, tradition

The King of Pentacles sits on their throne, looking down at the Pentacle on their lap. Their downward gaze symbolizes an orientation toward the material realm.

In their left hand, the king holds a scepter with a round globe at the top. The ornate throne is adorned with bulls in a nod to the earth sign of Taurus. Plants surround the king and the grapes decorating their cloak symbolize the abundance of the harvest.

There are blue mountains in the background, representing wisdom and achievement. There is a wall behind them and a castle beyond denoting human-made structures and tradition. The King of Pentacles is concerned with society, structure, security, and achievement.

This king likes quality and comfort. They also like security and routine. They may seem boring, but not if you look closely.

The King of Pentacles may be concerned with pragmatic matters such as farming or real estate. They like structure and work well in IT, law or any kind of engineering, building, or accounting.

The King of Pentacles is physically oriented and probably has an exercise routine. They are hard-working and spend their money wisely. They may not want to go to breakfast because they think it's overpriced, yet will happily spend money for dinner at a top-notch restaurant.

The King of Pentacles will dedicate their life to providing security for their family. They want their kids to grow up and to fend for themselves.

If this is your father, you better turn off the lights when you leave the room and close the door quickly if the air conditioning is on, although it will have to be pretty hot before the air conditioning can be justified. You likely know exactly how much the food cost that you didn't finish eating and you'll be expected to do your chores every day.

The King of Pentacles will organize the family to go biking together and do other character-building or healthy endeavors. There is little tolerance for activities which don't provide measurable benefit.

The King of Pentacles father will be proud of your achievements and will buy you the highest quality bat or electric guitar, but only if you need it. And they will probably use a coupon. They will be at every game and will tell you how you could improve. If you can hear their advice without getting your feelings hurt, it's quite helpful.

REVERSED KING OF PENTACLES

Dogmatic, miser, rigid, stubborn, boring, conventional, prejudiced

All the kings and queens, when reversed, can have issues with money. The King of Pentacles reversed is prone to imbalance around money. There can be a Scrooge motif, caring more about money and the illusion of security than humanity.

You'll probably want to avoid political discussions with the reversed King of Pentacles. They can be stubborn and rigidly set in their beliefs, certain they are right and not open to new ideas.

The King of Pentacles may judge others based on their income or titles. They can be attached to their creature comforts and routines. With the earth element out of balance, they have the potential to be overly concerned with appearances or fixated on health. There can be a tendency to control others in order to feel more secure.

Feelings may be a source of annoyance to the King of Pentacles. This is the parent you dread telling you want to major in theater. Approval will be unlikely. They might only begrudgingly come around after you win an Academy Award.

When out of balance, the King of Pentacles as a parent can be very controlling and limiting. There is little tolerance for anything outside of the norm and no room for dreaming, imagination or feelings.

The King of Pentacles reversed may be immovable, like a rock. They may be unable to go with the flow or to be innovative. It may be hard to get them to leave the comfort of their home.

ACTIVATING THE KING OF PENTACLES

The King of Pentacles is the ultimate business person. Invoke the king to help you understand the nature of money and commerce.

Is it time to grow up your relationship with money?

KING OF SWORDS

Elements: Earth & Air

Intelligent, analytical, discerning, judicious, rational

The King of Swords faces straight ahead, holding a sword in their right hand. They wear a blue robe and a mantle of purple. Their stone throne is engraved with butterflies and there are clouds and two birds soaring in the background.

The King of Swords is cool, calm, and collected. This king knows the answer and can cite studies to back it up. This is the doctor you want to have managing your case because they will know the groundbreaking research and be able to apply what is the best practice specifically as it relates to you.

Attraction for the King of Swords will begin with intellectual rapport. They will help solve your problems, but may be short on empathy. You'll want the King of Cups if you're looking for sensitivity.

The King of Swords is fair, never allowing sentimentality to cloud their judgment. Tony Stark, also known as Iron Man from Marvel comics is a good example.

The King of Swords as a parent may feel distant or detached. They may hold a baby awkwardly, but once language and intellectual development kicks in, they will be all in. And you can bet their kid's robotics team will take first place.

While the love is there with the King of Swords parent, it may not be as obvious. They may see their kids objectively because that's how they engage with life. They're probably not going to gush and cuddle, but they will be at every band concert.

This is the parent with whom you'll enjoy many discussions, religion and politics included. They can be a valuable source of sage counsel and advice.

The King of Swords will talk through problems with you and give expert advice. They will seek to understand your point of view. Their brilliance may express itself through humor and they can be a great wit.

REVERSED KING OF SWORDS

Aloof, harsh, intolerant, emotionally detached, calculating, rigid thinking

When reversed, the King of Swords can be overly analytical, emotionally detached, and even robotic. They can wield their intelligence like a sword to avoid intimacy. Or they can mask their insecurity with intellectual bravado.

The sword reversed represents a misused weapon. It could be intelligence untempered with heart, which could be critical or judgmental. Or it could be someone who always needs to be right or likes to argue. The King of Swords humor may be cutting or they may always need to win an argument, regardless of the damage to the relationship.

As a parent, the child could feel cut down by their sword or imprisoned by their rules. You may feel more like a lab experiment than a child. You may feel under scrutiny and subject to criticism. It may be hard for this king to allow you to have your own independent thoughts and life.

The King of Swords reversed could also represent a person with a lot of ideas but no substance or follow through. Or they could live in their head. They may not think before they charge ahead or may flit from one endeavor to another without completing.

ACTIVATING THE KING OF SWORDS

Many people go into a legal process expecting to be vindicated. They expect an authority to recognize their suffering and validate them. But it doesn't work that way. The law doesn't care. It can't.

The King of Swords is great at taking sentimentality out of the equation in order to see what is fair.

Is there any problem in your life that would benefit from some strategy or a spreadsheet?

———

KING OF CUPS

Elements: Earth & Water

Creative, magnetic, benevolent, compassionate, supportive

The King of Cups sits on a throne, looking slightly to the left, displaying an openness to emotion and creativity. The king has a cup in their right hand and a scepter in their left. They wear the fish from the page's cup and the knight's tunic on a chain around their neck, showing the incorporation of the subconscious into their expression.

The throne is rounded, suggesting comfort, sensitivity and the softer side of masculine consciousness with an awareness of feminine aspects of consciousness.

Like the King of Pentacles and the Emperor, the King of Cup's feet poke out from under their robes, but unlike the King of Pentacles and the Emperor, they don't appear to be wearing armor, signifying that their source of power doesn't come from force, but emanates from their heart-centered authority.

In the background and all around the king, is wavy water with a ship and a dolphin poking its head out of the water. The King of Cups has mastery over the water. Like the captain of a ship, they know how to work in harmony with the element of water in its many forms.

Their robe is blue under the yellow cloak, symbolizing a balance of emotion, intellect and spirit. Their green scaly shoes symbolize their ability to bridge water and earth.

Magnetic and attractive, this king will be in tune with you. Sex with them will probably include the emotional and energetic bodies. They are plugged in spiritually and have the potential to operate at a high level of awareness.

This king is intuitive and often clairvoyant with a rich dream life and may be psychic and prophetic. The King of Cups could represent artists of all mediums.

The King of Cups can be a wonderfully devoted and nurturing parent. They'll probably be very involved, especially when the kids are little. They and the baby may snuggle up for naps and they may delight in feeding the baby.

Like the Queen of Cups, the King of Cups may love having someone totally dependent on them for nurturance and care-giving. With a little being who can't reject or abandon them, it's safe for them to pour out all of their love. They may prefer to be a primary care-giver and will be very in tune with the child's needs.

It can be hard for the King of Cups to allow their children to grow up. The teenage years may be challenging, as the child needs to separate and define themselves.

REVERSED KING OF CUPS

Melodrama, temperamental, passive-aggressive, fantasy, manipulation

Blocked or frozen water can't flow, so when the King of Cups is reversed, there can be an inability to deal with reality. This inability may manifest as addiction, dishonesty, weight, depression, anxiety, or defensiveness to cover up insecurity.

When a cup turns upside down, it empties and seeks to be filled. As a result, the King of Cups can be needy, controlling and manipulating, easily fusing with or smothering others in codependent relationships, latching on to life energy. Other sources may be sought to fill the empty cup, such as sex, alcohol, or drugs.

When reversed, the king may simper or fawn. Or they could be vindictive if they felt jaded. Their emotions may be out of balance, making them prone to melodrama. They may be hypersensitive or delusional, having a very fluid and self-serving definition of "truth". They can justify anything if it serves them and they will believe their own lies.

When reversed, the King of Cups can be slippery. They can be emotionally or psychologically manipulative and possibly bullying. It may be so subtle you don't realize it until your self-esteem has disintegrated and you no longer remember who you are.

All the kings and queens have stalker potential when out of balance, but the King of Cups is a prime candidate for having difficulty letting go of a romantic relationship.

When the King of Cups is reversed, it can denote immaturity or stunted growth. They may not be able to say "no", particularly to their parents and family of origin.

As a parent, there is a strong potential to latch onto the child as a source and to smother the child. This can confuse the child, since on the surface, the behaviors appear to be loving.

An imbalanced King of Cups can become jealous and compete with their children for attention, becoming a child themselves, which is not a healthy dynamic for a partnership.

ACTIVATING THE KING OF CUPS

It takes a lot of energy to build walls or to hold a grudge. The King of Cups can remind you that an open heart is a strong heart. Ideally, we want to walk into a room and feel only loving neutrality, no matter who is in the room.

Is there any person in your life with whom you don't have loving neutrality? How could you get to loving neutrality?

———

KING OF WANDS

Elements: Earth & Fire

Entrepreneurial, drive, will, dynamic, innovative

The king sits on a throne in the desert, facing to the right with their wand held upright in their right hand like a scepter. Salamanders decorate their yellow cloak, symbolizing the purifying and restorative quality of fire.

The prongs of their crown resemble flames, further emphasizing the element of fire as it relates to power and to the intellect. Lions and salamanders decorate the back of their throne and a salamander basks in the sun at the base of their throne.

The King of Wands is the personification of fire. When upright, you want to party with this person or go see them perform live on the main stage. They are dynamic, adventurous, hilarious, and everything is exciting when they're around.

As a parent, the King of Wands is generous, playful, and protective. They can be counted on to fiercely protect their home and their family. They may never see a fault in their children and will always look for new ways to help or to motivate them.

The King of Wands knows how to make things happen. They can be intense and they have a lot of initiative, energy, and ideas. They're motivating, encouraging, competitive, and they aren't afraid to take action.

This card could represent many professional athletes and successful entrepreneurs, but they could be in any type of work, especially where they can be a leader or a star.

REVERSED KING OF WANDS

Controlling, dramatic, argumentative, rebellious, thrill-seeking

There are two ways to think of the King of Wands reversed. The first is too much fire, like a wildfire. The second is not enough fire, like the Lion in the Wizard of Oz.

When fire is out of control, there is rage, destruction, and abuse of power. This often manifests as imposing personal will on others which can appear selfish, disrespectful, and inconsiderate to the other parties.

The King of Wands reversed can be a dominating dictator who is ego-centric, bossy, impatient, intimidating, angry, or just plain annoying.

When you're dealing with an imbalanced King of Wands, there can be little regard for the truth or for the welfare of others. With too much fire, the King of Wands can burn themselves out through overwork, being an adrenaline junkie, extreme competition, panic disorders, anxiety, addiction, excessive work or exercise. They can also scatter their fire, due to lack of focus.

When there is not enough fire, it can manifest as a deep fear and insecurity covered up with bravado. They may feel the need to be excessively in control of themselves and of others, such as jealousy, possessiveness, or being overly protective.

Without enough fire, it can mean the person represented by the King of Wands reversed is depressed or stuck. There can be a lack of motivation or libido. Or a lot of smoke, but no fire, meaning a lot of promises with no actual results.

When reversed, there is usually an abuse of power somewhere, either externalized as controlling others in order to feel secure, or else internalized and manifesting as disorders such as OCD or a lack of confidence, drive, or determination.

Imbalanced fire can also express an extreme need for order and fastidiousness. It may also appear as a need to be the center of attention, needing to be right, or needing to win at all costs.

As a parent, the King of Wands may prefer a more extroverted and expressive child who is obedient. Like their brethren kings of pentacles and swords, their tolerance could be low for other people's emotions.

An imbalanced King of Wands may regard their children as an audience or as a reflection of themself. They may not remember that it is the kid playing on the field and not them. The reversed King of Wands is the parent who gets banned from attending their kids' games for challenging the ref.

The King of Wands father, when reversed, can be selfish and intolerant. They may be stuck in a teenager mentality and rebel against their partner, or unconsciously compete with their children for attention. They may have a hard time understanding the needs of others, especially when their needs are an inconvenience to them.

AWAKENING THE KING OF WANDS

The King of Wands is a natural trailblazer. You can invoke the King of Wands when you need to get things fired up. Like fire, they can purify and cleanse, leaving clarity and decisive action.

What in your life needs to be purified by fire?

Conclusion

The true power of tarot is the development of self-awareness as a tool for transforming your life. And the ultimate reason for this study is to develop a greater capacity for love.

Ideally, your journey through the 78 cards has helped you remember what you already knew. By engaging with the cards and accessing tarot's ancient wisdom, you can find a deeper understanding of universal life lessons and every experience you have can grant you access to higher realms of consciousness.

Now that you've opened the door of your subconscious, the cards will continue to unveil their secrets, waking up your heart and shedding light in your life.

As you've worked your way through the cards and the cards have worked their way through you, I hope they changed your world. I hope you feel differently about your relationship with life, love, the universe, and everything.

I hope that you have been touched by earth, air, water and fire and that you could slow dance with the Empress, take a risk with the Fool, befriend the Tower, and that you reconnected with your Star that you will bring to the world.

As you continue journeying with tarot, I invite you to surrender to this process. These lessons will continue revealing themselves to you, and this book can provide you with a strong container for this ongoing discovery.

Card Spreads

Three-Card Spreads

Working with too many cards in the beginning can be overwhelming and less effective. The Three-Card spread is the easiest way to start.

Here's how you do it:

1. Shuffle the deck and then draw three cards.
2. Place the first card in the center. This card represents the main issue, concern, or state of mind right now.

3. Place the second card to the left of the first card. This card represents the recent past or what influences contributed to the current state illustrated by the first card.

4. Place the third card to the right of the first card. This card represents the future, next step or likely outcome if the current course is continued.

———

THE PROBLEM-SOLVING SPREAD

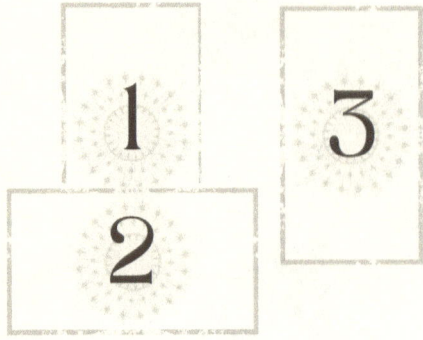

1. Problem
2. Cause
3. Solution

RELATIONSHIP CLARIFICATION SPREAD

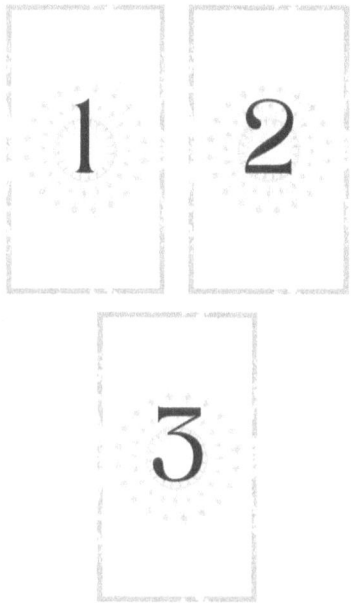

1. You
2. The Other Person
3. The Relationship

YES/NO SPREAD

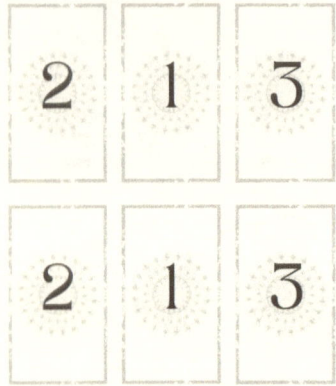

A Yes-No spread is best employed when there are two clear paths of choice.

Most situations in life aren't black and white and the Yes/No spread will rarely tell you exactly what to do, but instead amplify and reflect the issues you're grappling with as you're trying to choose. Often, looking at the yes-no options will lead to more questions or will generate alternatives that weren't imagined before.

1. For the Yes part of the spread, ask: "Is it for my highest good to _____?"
2. Then you draw three cards, beginning with the center card, then a card to the left, then a card to the right.
3. For the No part of the spread, ask, "Is it for my highest good *not* to _____?"
4. Then you draw three cards again in the manner described above and place them either above or below the line of "yes" cards that you just drew.
5. The quality of the cards and the upright or reversed position will usually answer your question if a clear answer can be known.

6. You'll want to look at the quality of the cards. Give more weight and pay more attention to any major arcana cards, and try to understand what the universe is telling you. The Devil card reversed, for example, is likely a "yes" while The Moon upright is a "maybe" but is telling you that there may be confusion or deeper topics at play such as subterfuge, delusion, or past lives.

LIKELY "YES" CARDS WHEN UPRIGHT:

- The Fool, The Magician, The Empress, The Emperor, The Hierophant, The Lovers, The Chariot, Strength, Wheel of Fortune, Justice, Temperance, The Star, The Sun, Judgment, The World
- All the Aces
- All the wands except: five, seven, nine and ten
- All the cups except: four, five, seven, eight
- All the pentacles except: two, four, five, seven
- Six, Page, Knight, Queen, King of Swords

LIKELY "NO" CARDS WHEN UPRIGHT

- The Devil, Death, The Tower
- Five, Seven, Eight, and Ten of Wands
- Five and Eight of Cups
- Three, Five, Seven, Eight, Nine, Ten of Swords
- Four and Five of Pentacles

MAYBE CARDS UPRIGHT OR REVERSED:

- The High Priestess, The Hermit, The Hanged Man, The Moon, The Tower, Death
- Four and Seven of Cups
- Two, Three and Four of Swords
- Two or Seven of Pentacles

CELTIC CROSS

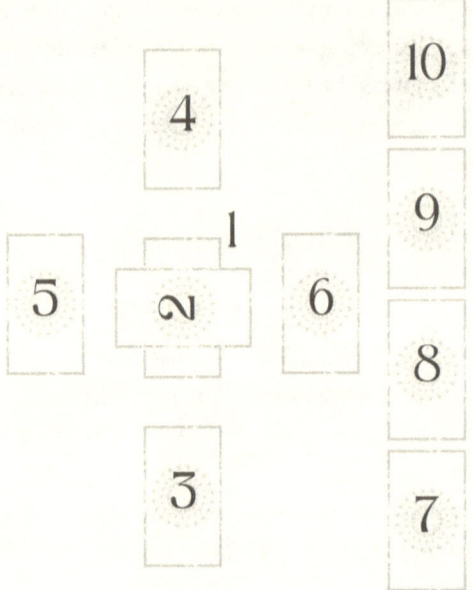

The Celtic Cross is the most common spread in tarot. This is a lot of cards all at once and can feel overwhelming when you're just beginning your tarot study. One, or three card spreads can be equally profound and usually the best place to start. There are quite a few variations to the Celtic Cross. What follows is how I use this spread.

- Card 1 The base card and central issue
- Card 2 What crosses you or challenges you
- Card 3 Subconscious influences
- Card 4 Conscious influences
- Card 5 Past influences
- Card 6 Future influences
- Card 7 Fear, avoidance
- Card 8 Other people
- Card 9 Hopes
- Card 10 Outcome

I pay the most attention to card 3, the subconscious contributing factors and to card 7, the fear card, as these are largely unconscious and the strongest drivers of the situation and therefore the most fruitful cards for exploration. From there I notice any major arcana as they will illuminate what major life lesson is at play.

Acknowledgments

For my parents, who gave me my first tarot deck and the love, encouragement, and freedom to find my way.

For my sister, who helped keep me awake and laughing during the hardest parts.

For my brother, for his belief in me and good questions.

For Marlene Delott, my first tarot teacher and spiritual mother, and my cousin, Rosalie, who first introduced me to tarot and later to Marlene.

For the wise and generous guidance of all my teachers.

For the friends, extended family, and fellow seekers who were instrumental in my healing and awakening.

I owe special gratitude to my dear clients and students throughout the years who were so frequently my teachers and whose tarot stories are contained in these pages.

Thanks to my editor and book midwife, Leah Kent, for her patience and skill ushering this book into print.

Biggest thanks of all to my daughters, Audrey and Aria, for the inspiration of their beings.

ABOUT THE AUTHOR

Laura is an energy shift expert. Using tarot, astrology, embodiment, and plant spirit medicine, Laura guides spiritual seekers to get unstuck, and in alignment in order to live a more purposeful life.

To learn more, visit laurashawconsulting.com

www.ingramcontent.com/pod-product-compliance
Lightning Source LLC
Chambersburg PA
CBHW030405130626
46549CB00004B/1643